How to Quit Alcohol

CRAFTED BY SKRIUWER

Copyright © 2024 by Skriuwer.

All rights reserved. No part of this book may be used or reproduced in any form whatsoever without written permission except in the case of brief quotations in critical articles or reviews.

For more information, contact : **kontakt@skriuwer.com** (www.skriuwer.com)

TABLE OF CONTENTS

CHAPTER 1: UNDERSTANDING ALCOHOL DEPENDENCE

- Basic definition of problem drinking and dependency
- Why physical and mental factors matter
- Different types of drinking patterns
- Early signs and common misconceptions

CHAPTER 2: PHYSICAL & CHEMICAL EFFECTS OF ALCOHOL

- How alcohol moves through the body
- Impact on brain, liver, heart, and other organs
- Withdrawal symptoms and their risks
- Long-term health changes from heavy use

CHAPTER 3: REAL REASONS BEHIND PROBLEM DRINKING

- Emotional triggers and hidden causes
- Environmental and social pressures
- Genetic factors and family influence
- Why early experiences shape drinking habits

CHAPTER 4: SETTING CLEAR GOALS FOR CHANGE

- Deciding between cutting down or quitting fully
- Creating SMART goals and tracking progress
- Building accountability and motivation
- Handling slips and staying focused

CHAPTER 5: PLANNING & PREPARING FOR A BETTER FUTURE

- Organizing your living space to reduce triggers
- Building daily routines and schedules
- Financial planning and saving money
- Communicating with housemates or family

CHAPTER 6: HANDLING WITHDRAWAL SAFELY

- Understanding mild to severe withdrawal
- Medical detox vs. home management
- Managing cravings, anxiety, and insomnia
- Building a support system during early recovery

CHAPTER 7: BUILDING A STRONG SUPPORT SYSTEM

- Choosing who to trust and lean on
- Types of support: emotional, informational, and more
- Handling unsupportive friends or family
- Finding in-person and online groups

CHAPTER 8: MANAGING STRESS & EMOTIONAL TRIGGERS

- Identifying emotional warning signs
- Healthy outlets for anxiety, anger, or sadness
- Practical relaxation techniques
- Replacing old coping habits with better ones

CHAPTER 9: PRACTICAL TIPS TO PREVENT SLIPS

- Recognizing early signals of relapse
- Planning for high-risk events or environments
- Coping with sudden urges and cravings
- Using a 'slips and solutions' journal

CHAPTER 10: BALANCED NUTRITION AND SELF-CARE

- Importance of replenishing nutrients
- Building a meal plan and hydration routine
- Light exercise and better sleep practices
- Personal grooming and mental well-being

CHAPTER 11: BUILDING NEW ROUTINES AND HOBBIES

- Replacing old drinking habits with healthy activities
- Finding interests for fun and growth
- Managing boredom and motivation dips
- Combining routines with personal passions

CHAPTER 12: HANDLING SOCIAL SITUATIONS AND PEER PRESSURE

- Polite ways to refuse drinks
- Navigating family events and work functions
- Dealing with teasing or criticism
- Social life without feeling left out

CHAPTER 13: LONG-TERM HEALTH CHECKS & BODY CHANGES

- Ongoing liver, heart, and brain recovery
- Medical checkups and monitoring improvements
- Physical and mental gains over time
- Detecting hidden issues early

CHAPTER 14: SPOTTING WARNING SIGNS OF PROBLEMS

- Mild slips vs. full setbacks
- Physical, emotional, and social red flags
- Handling financial or work stress signals
- Quick action steps when trouble appears

CHAPTER 15: HELPING OTHERS AND SHARING ADVICE

- Why supporting others can strengthen your own resolve
- Balancing personal boundaries with offering help
- Practical tips for guiding friends or family
- Encouraging professional support or group programs

CHAPTER 16: MOVING ON FROM PAST MISTAKES

- Difference between guilt and shame
- Self-forgiveness and making amends
- Rebuilding identity beyond old habits
- Overcoming resentment and regret

CHAPTER 17: STAYING MOTIVATED IN DAILY LIFE

- Refreshing goals when enthusiasm fades
- Small daily tactics to keep motivation alive
- Using short-term rewards and checking in with yourself
- Avoiding complacency and overconfidence

CHAPTER 18: FINANCIAL AND LEGAL CONCERNS

- Budgeting and tracking alcohol savings
- Handling debt, fines, or court orders
- Employment issues tied to past alcohol use
- Long-term financial planning and stability

CHAPTER 19: ADVANCED TIPS FOR UNCOMMON PROBLEMS

- Living with a heavy-drinking partner
- Rare medical or allergy-related issues
- Remote living with limited support
- Managing triggers in high-pressure fields

CHAPTER 20: LOOKING FORWARD AND STAYING ON TRACK

- Ongoing growth and adapting to life changes
- Maintaining health, relationships, and financial goals
- Handling relapses or unexpected stresses
- Finding deeper purpose and keeping momentum

CHAPTER 1: UNDERSTANDING ALCOHOL DEPENDENCE

Alcohol dependence is a condition where a person feels an ongoing need to drink. This need can feel so strong that it affects everyday life. People in this situation often find it hard to control how much they drink or how often they drink. Some might try to stop, only to feel strong cravings that lead them back to the bottle. In this chapter, we will cover the basic facts about problem drinking, the roots of this behavior, and the reasons why it becomes such a deep problem for many people. We will also explore how family background, emotional factors, and hidden elements in a person's life can merge to bring about dependence. By the end of this chapter, you will have a clear idea of how alcohol dependence develops and why it can take hold.

1.1 A Basic Explanation of Alcohol Dependence

Alcohol dependence goes beyond just liking a drink now and then. It involves a pattern of craving and loss of control. Some people might start off drinking at social events, such as backyard cookouts or after-work gatherings. With time, the drinking can become more frequent or heavier. A person might begin to rely on alcohol to cope with stress or negative thoughts.

When dependence takes hold, a person's brain can start to adapt to regular alcohol intake. They might feel like they need alcohol to handle everyday tasks. Some cannot start their day without a drink. Others need a drink to relax before bed. Over time, this pattern can become hard to break. Dependence means the brain and body have grown so used to alcohol that they respond with discomfort or strong cravings when it is not present.

It is important to note that not everyone who drinks daily is dependent. Some people might have a daily habit but are still able to reduce or skip drinking if needed. True dependence is often marked by physical and emotional symptoms that happen when a person tries to cut down or stop drinking.

Why It Is Important to Understand Dependence

When you understand how alcohol dependence forms, you can see that it is not just about willpower. There are real changes in the body and brain that make it hard to stop. Knowing the reasons behind these changes can reduce feelings of shame and self-blame. People who are aware of how dependence works often find it easier to accept that they need help and medical attention for their condition.

1.2 Different Types of Drinkers

Not everyone who drinks regularly is the same. Experts might talk about various "types" of drinkers to better describe behavior patterns.

1. **Social Drinkers**: These individuals only drink at special events or when out with friends. They might have a couple of beers or glasses of wine and stop without issues. They do not experience withdrawal symptoms and do not rely on alcohol to feel okay.
2. **Binge Drinkers**: People who drink a large amount of alcohol in a short span of time. They do not necessarily drink every day, but when they do, they might consume a lot. This can lead to harmful effects like blackouts or risky behavior.
3. **Heavy Regular Drinkers**: They drink a fair amount most days. They might not face severe problems at first, but their body and mind can be at risk over time. They could develop a tolerance, meaning they need more alcohol to feel the same effect.
4. **Dependent Drinkers**: They have a strong physical or mental need for alcohol. These individuals might experience shaky hands or strong cravings if they go too long without a drink. Stopping or even cutting down can lead to withdrawal symptoms.

Seeing these different categories can help you figure out where you stand. This is not meant to label or shame anyone. Rather, it helps pinpoint the level of risk and what steps might be needed next.

1.3 Roots of Alcohol Dependence

Dependence can have many roots. It can begin with social surroundings, genetics, emotional struggles, or even physical reactions to alcohol.

1. **Genetics**: Research shows that genes can play a part in the risk for alcohol dependence. If a close relative had serious drinking problems, this might raise the chance that you could have similar issues. However, it is not set in stone. Genetics only increase the risk; they do not decide your fate.
2. **Environment**: Growing up in a home where heavy drinking is common can lead some to see drinking as normal. Stressful life settings, high-pressure jobs, or chaotic home lives can push people toward using alcohol as a coping method.
3. **Emotional Health**: Individuals who battle sadness, anxiety, or other conditions might use alcohol to soften overwhelming emotions. Over time, they can get stuck in a cycle of self-medicating. This can lead to a physical or mental need for alcohol.
4. **Early Exposure**: People who start drinking at a young age can be more likely to develop harmful patterns later in life. Early exposure can teach the brain to expect alcohol as part of daily living.
5. **Stress and Trauma**: A major factor for many is the presence of stress or past events that were upsetting. Alcohol might feel like a shortcut to numb thoughts or worries. Over time, this short-term fix can become a long-term trap.

1.4 Early Signs and Indicators

It is crucial to spot the warning signs of dependence. These signs can appear slowly. Some people might look back and realize their habits changed over months or years.

1. **Needing More Alcohol**: Tolerance is a red flag. If you find that you need larger amounts than before to get the same feeling, this can mean your body is growing used to the substance.
2. **Cravings**: A powerful urge to drink, especially at times of stress, can be a clue. People might think about the next drink to calm themselves.
3. **Hiding Drinking Habits**: If you find yourself hiding bottles, lying about how much you drink, or sneaking in drinks without others knowing, it often signals you feel shame or fear about your behavior.
4. **Feeling Guilty**: Many people with dependence feel guilt or shame after drinking. They might promise to quit tomorrow but fail to do so.

5. **Skipping Other Activities**: You might start avoiding hobbies, outings, or other events so you can drink instead. In some cases, the person loses interest in things they once cared about.
6. **Withdrawal Symptoms**: Shaky hands, sweating, nervousness, and trouble sleeping when not drinking can be signs that your body is used to alcohol. If these symptoms stop when you have a drink, it is a strong sign of dependence.

1.5 Myths About Alcohol Dependence

Myth 1: "Only people who drink all day can be dependent."
Fact: Someone can seem fine during the day but still be reliant on alcohol at night. Dependence is not always obvious from the outside.

Myth 2: "You have to hit rock bottom before you can change."
Fact: Many people choose to stop or reduce drinking before severe problems occur. Early action is often easier and more effective.

Myth 3: "It is just a matter of willpower."
Fact: While choice does play a role, the body and mind both change when dependence sets in. This is a health issue, not simply a lack of self-discipline.

Myth 4: "Cutting down is enough."
Fact: Some people can manage by reducing. Others need to quit fully. The correct path can depend on health factors and how serious the dependence is.

1.6 Long-Term Risks of Ignoring Dependence

Some people put off dealing with problem drinking because they feel it is not a major issue right now. But ignoring dependence can lead to serious harms:

1. **Liver Damage**: Long-term heavy drinking can harm the liver. This can lead to permanent scarring known as cirrhosis, which can be life-threatening.
2. **Heart Problems**: Alcohol can affect the heart by causing irregular rhythms or weakening the heart muscle. High blood pressure is also linked to heavy drinking.

3. **Brain Changes**: Alcohol can impact brain function, changing mood and memory. Over time, it can lead to a reduced ability to think clearly or even permanent brain damage in serious cases.
4. **Relationship Strains**: People who struggle with alcohol often have conflicts with family and friends. Unpredictable behavior can weaken trust.
5. **Work and Financial Trouble**: Many individuals who are dependent on alcohol have missed workdays, poor performance, or job loss. They might use their money for drinks instead of bills, leading to serious financial stress.

1.7 Hidden Social and Emotional Costs

Beyond health problems, alcohol dependence can lead to issues that are not always obvious. One might notice a drop in self-esteem, a feeling of isolation, or a loss of personal identity. Many people feel guilty about their actions when drinking, which can feed negative thoughts. There is also the risk of legal trouble if someone drinks and drives. As these burdens grow, quitting can feel more and more daunting.

Some unique problems can arise for certain groups:

1. **Parents**: Drinking problems can affect a person's ability to look after children. It can strain the bond with their children. Over time, children might develop emotional issues from the unstable atmosphere.
2. **Older Adults**: Seniors can have a hard time handling alcohol because their bodies do not break it down as easily. They might also mix alcohol with medications, leading to health dangers.
3. **Students or Young Adults**: If drinking becomes a habit in early adult life, it might slow academic progress, harm social relationships, or set patterns that are tough to break later.

1.8 Personal Responsibility and Getting Ready for a Shift

It is helpful to know that if you are reading this, you have already taken a vital step. Being aware of a problem and wanting to learn about it is a key turning point. Alcohol dependence does not have to define you. Many have been in the same situation and have found ways to move forward. You can do the same with the right knowledge and support.

Shifting from problem drinking to a more stable life involves learning, making a plan, and seeking help if needed. One should consider health factors and emotional well-being. This is a big undertaking that requires steady effort. Remember, making the decision to improve is often the hardest step. The rest involves learning methods and using resources available.

1.9 Little-Known Facts and Extra Insights

Most people know that heavy drinking can be bad for the liver or lead to blackouts. But there are many hidden insights that can help you see the bigger picture:

1. **Brain Chemistry Influence**: Alcohol affects parts of the brain tied to self-control and decision-making. When a person drinks regularly, the changes in brain chemicals can lower inhibitions, making them behave in ways they would not normally choose.
2. **Genetic Markers**: While having a close relative who struggles with alcohol can increase your risk, there are actual markers in your genes that might be linked to how your body breaks down alcohol. This can affect how quickly you feel drunk or how strongly you crave more.
3. **Cross-Tolerance with Other Substances**: If someone is dependent on alcohol, they might find that they can handle certain medications differently than those who do not drink. This is known as cross-tolerance. It means the body is used to certain effects, which can alter how a person responds to other drugs.
4. **Hidden Impact on Hormones**: Alcohol can affect hormone levels. Over time, this can lead to changes in how the body manages stress, hunger, or even sexual function. These shifts can fuel a cycle of drinking, because the body's own internal balances are off.
5. **Changes in Sleep Patterns**: Many people think a drink at night helps them sleep, but it can worsen the quality of rest. Alcohol might make a person fall asleep faster, but it can reduce deep sleep, leaving them tired the next day. This can lead to more drinking for "energy," increasing dependence.

1.10 Self-Reflection Exercise

While you read this book, it can help to pause and check in with yourself. Think about the following:

- **Daily Habits**: Write down how often you think about drinking. Has it become a part of routines (like finishing the day or calming stress)?
- **Motives for Drinking**: Ask why you feel you need alcohol. Is it to block out a memory, calm your nerves, or keep up with friends?
- **Feelings After Drinking**: Do you regret your actions, or do you feel like you "must" do it again?
- **Physical Symptoms**: Have you noticed shaking, sweating, or a racing heart when you skip drinks?

This type of thinking can give you vital clues about your pattern. Knowledge of your own behaviors and feelings is an important step toward change.

1.11 Preparing Mentally

Even before making a formal plan to cut down or quit, a good first step is to prepare your mind. Some people start by doing small experiments, like skipping a drink for one day to see how they feel. Others try tracking their drinks in a journal. By noticing triggers and times of high stress, you can gain valuable data about what drives your behavior.

If you find you cannot skip drinking without distress, that does not mean you have failed. It suggests that your body and mind are adjusting in a way that might need medical or professional help. This knowledge is useful as you move forward.

1.12 Common Misunderstandings

- **"I only drink on weekends, so it cannot be that bad."**
  Some weekend drinkers consume very large amounts in a short time, which can be risky. This pattern can still result in dependence over time.
- **"I can stop whenever I want."**
  Many people believe they can stop. But once they try, they realize the body and mind react strongly, showing that dependence has formed.

- **"Alcohol helps me cope with stress."**
  In the short term, alcohol might lower tension. But in the long term, it adds more stress (health problems, financial issues, and strained relationships).

1.13 How Society Influences Dependence

Media and advertising often depict alcohol in fun ways. Popular culture might show drinking as a normal part of hanging out with friends. This can mislead people into thinking that heavy drinking is without risk. TV shows might show characters who rely on alcohol, passing it off as common or harmless.

Family influence is also huge. If children grow up watching parents deal with stress by drinking, they might copy that behavior when they face their own problems. Social surroundings can add to the challenge of quitting, because many events and gatherings revolve around alcohol.

CHAPTER 2: PHYSICAL AND CHEMICAL EFFECTS OF ALCOHOL

In this chapter, we will look at what happens inside your body when you drink. Alcohol affects organs, hormones, and brain chemicals in a unique way. Many people are aware that long-term drinking can harm the liver. But there is more to it than that. We will examine how alcohol interacts with different body parts, how it can lead to specific health conditions, and why cutting down or quitting can be so challenging once dependence has formed. Knowing this science can give you a stronger sense of why you feel or behave a certain way when drinking.

2.1 How Alcohol Travels Through the Body

When you take a sip of beer, wine, or liquor, alcohol travels quickly into your bloodstream. Here is a basic path:

1. **Mouth and Stomach**: Some alcohol is absorbed in the stomach. If you have food in your stomach, it can slow down the absorption rate.
2. **Small Intestine**: Most absorption takes place here. Once alcohol hits the small intestine, it passes into the bloodstream.
3. **Liver**: The liver processes alcohol, breaking it down with enzymes. One of the main enzymes is called alcohol dehydrogenase. The liver can handle only a certain amount of alcohol per hour. Anything above that limit builds up in the bloodstream.
4. **Brain**: Alcohol in the blood goes to the brain. It affects messages between brain cells, slowing them down. This leads to the familiar effects such as feeling less inhibited or less coordinated.

2.2 Effects on the Brain and Nerves

One of the main reasons people develop dependence is the effect that alcohol has on the brain. Alcohol influences chemical messengers like gamma-aminobutyric acid (GABA) and glutamate. This can create a chain reaction of feeling relaxed or somewhat uplifted. But as time passes, the brain adapts. Here is a look at the details:

1. **Dopamine Release**: Alcohol can cause a release of dopamine, which is a messenger linked to pleasure. This is partly why you might feel good after a drink. When the alcohol is gone, the body wants that feeling again, so you might crave another drink.
2. **Slowed Reactions**: Alcohol suppresses certain brain functions, slowing reaction times and hurting coordination. Over time, heavy use can weaken memory and other mental tasks.
3. **Mood Changes**: Some people feel happy or calm after a drink. Others might become angry or sad. This variation depends on personal chemistry, mood before drinking, and overall mental health.
4. **Loss of Inhibitions**: A few drinks can make people take risks they normally would not. This might include driving, getting into fights, or using other substances.
5. **Physical Dependence**: With repeated exposure, the brain can come to expect alcohol in order to regulate chemistry. If a person suddenly stops, the body might react with shaking, anxiety, or seizures.

2.3 Impact on the Liver

The liver is the main organ for processing alcohol. When you drink heavily or often, the liver can become overloaded. Eventually, this can lead to liver diseases:

1. **Fatty Liver**: This is an early sign that the liver is having trouble. Fat deposits build up around liver cells. If a person stops drinking at this stage, the liver can often repair itself.
2. **Hepatitis**: Heavy drinking can cause inflammation in the liver. This can be short-term or long-term. Long-term inflammation can lead to scarring.
3. **Cirrhosis**: This is severe scarring of the liver. Scar tissue replaces healthy cells. The liver might fail to do its job, which can cause a buildup of toxins in the blood.
4. **Liver Failure**: In some cases, the liver can reach a point of failing to function. This can be life-threatening.

Why the Liver Matters: The liver helps clean the blood, break down toxins, and support digestion. When it does not work well, a person's overall health can drop quickly. Many individuals with advanced liver problems might show yellowing of the skin (jaundice), swelling in the abdomen, and other issues. Early detection and cutting down or quitting can prevent these serious conditions.

2.4 Harm to the Heart

Alcohol affects the heart and blood vessels too. Some major risks:

1. **High Blood Pressure**: Heavy drinking can cause spikes in blood pressure. Over time, this adds strain to the heart and vessels.
2. **Irregular Heartbeats**: Some people develop irregular rhythms like atrial fibrillation, which can lead to complications such as blood clots.
3. **Cardiomyopathy**: This is a weakening of the heart muscle. The heart may not pump blood effectively, leading to fatigue, shortness of breath, and serious health problems.
4. **Stroke Risk**: If you have high blood pressure or an irregular heartbeat due to alcohol, it can raise the chance of having a stroke. This can cause permanent brain damage.

2.5 Effects on the Digestive System

Drinking can damage the digestive tract in multiple ways:

1. **Irritation of the Stomach**: Alcohol can irritate the stomach lining, leading to acid reflux or ulcers. This can cause heartburn or pain after eating or drinking.
2. **Malnutrition**: Heavy drinkers might skip meals or get fewer nutrients from their diet. Alcohol also blocks the absorption of certain vitamins and minerals.
3. **Pancreatitis**: The pancreas plays a key role in digestion and insulin production. Long-term drinking can cause inflammation of the pancreas (pancreatitis), leading to pain and digestion problems.

2.6 Body Weight and Metabolism

Some people say they gain weight if they drink too much beer or sugary cocktails. Alcohol contains empty calories, meaning it adds to your daily intake without providing useful nutrients. Also, drinking can slow down the body's ability to burn fat. Here are some details:

1. **Increased Fat Storage**: The body treats alcohol as a poison. It focuses on breaking down alcohol first, which can slow normal fat-burning processes.
2. **Sugar in Mixed Drinks**: Many mixed drinks have soda or juice, which adds extra calories. This can lead to weight gain and problems like high blood sugar.
3. **Skipping Healthy Meals**: People who drink heavily sometimes skip meals. They replace food with alcohol. But their body does not receive the vitamins and minerals it needs, which can cause further health problems over time.

2.7 Immune System and Infection Risks

Fewer people realize that heavy drinking weakens the immune system. Over time, the body's ability to fight infection drops. This can lead to frequent colds, cases of flu, or other infections. Alcohol can also reduce the number of white blood cells, which are crucial for fighting off diseases.

2.8 Changes in Hormone Balance

Alcohol can throw off the body's hormone levels. This includes hormones tied to stress, metabolism, and other vital functions. For instance, long-term drinking can reduce testosterone in men and increase the risk of fertility problems. In women, it might interrupt menstrual cycles. Hormone imbalances can lead to mood swings, changes in energy levels, and other issues.

2.9 Brain Chemistry and Withdrawal Symptoms

The human brain has a delicate balance of messengers that control mood, muscle movements, and thought processes. Over time, alcohol use can shift this balance. When a dependent person quits drinking, the sudden drop in alcohol can lead to withdrawal symptoms.

1. **Mild Symptoms**: Shakes, headaches, anxiety, and sweating.

2. **Moderate Symptoms**: Irregular heartbeats, trouble focusing, nausea, and vomiting.
3. **Severe Symptoms (Delirium Tremens)**: Hallucinations, seizures, confusion, and extreme agitation. This condition can be life-threatening.

Withdrawal is one reason why many people find quitting so tough. The body has come to expect alcohol in its chemical mix. Without it, the brain sends distress signals.

2.10 Sleep Disruption

Many rely on a nightcap to fall asleep. But alcohol can hurt the quality of rest. While it might help with falling asleep, it disrupts the body's normal sleep cycles. Deep rest gets cut short, so a person might feel tired the next day. This can cause a cycle of using alcohol to relax, then dealing with fatigue, which can lead to more drinking.

2.11 Emotional Consequences and the Science Behind Them

Heavy drinking can worsen or trigger issues like sadness, anxiety, or anger. The chemical changes in the brain might cause a person to overreact to normal stressors. This can mean arguments at home or trouble at work. When people feel bad afterward, they might drink more to reduce the guilt.

Important Point: Once the brain links alcohol to relief from negative emotions, it can become a primary coping method. This process can be hard to reverse and often needs outside help.

2.12 Less Common Physical Problems

Many know about liver damage, but there are other, less talked-about problems caused by heavy drinking:

1. **Skin Issues**: Alcohol can dehydrate the skin, making it look dull or causing flushing (red face). Over time, some drinkers notice facial redness or broken capillaries on the nose and cheeks.

2. **Bone Health**: Excessive drinking can affect how the body uses calcium and vitamin D, which are important for bone strength. Weak bones can lead to fractures.
3. **Nerve Damage**: Known as neuropathy, this can cause tingling, numbness, or pain in the hands and feet. It happens because alcohol damages the nerves over time.

2.13 Alcohol and the Mind-Body Link

The mind and body are closely linked. When the body is harmed by alcohol, mental health suffers. At the same time, when the mind is distressed, it can trigger physical symptoms. This back-and-forth can create a cycle. For instance, a person who feels extreme anxiety might drink to calm themselves, but the next day their anxiety returns even stronger because alcohol changes brain chemicals. This sets off another round of drinking.

2.14 Dangerous Mixing of Substances

Mixing alcohol with other substances can be risky:

1. **Painkillers**: Many are processed by the liver. Adding alcohol puts extra strain on this organ, possibly leading to overdose or severe liver harm.
2. **Benzodiazepines (Anti-Anxiety Medications)**: Mixing these with alcohol can lead to extreme drowsiness, slowed breathing, or even coma.
3. **Opioids**: The combination with alcohol raises the risk of breathing problems and overdose.

If you have been dependent on alcohol, discuss any medications with a medical professional to avoid dangerous interactions.

2.15 Unique Points About Tolerance

People often talk about tolerance as if it is the same for everyone. But tolerance has different forms:

1. **Metabolic Tolerance**: The liver gets faster at breaking down alcohol, so you do not feel the effects as much at first.

2. **Functional Tolerance**: The brain and body adapt to operate with alcohol present. You might not look drunk, but the substance is still affecting organs.
3. **Acute Tolerance**: This can happen quickly, even within a single drinking session. Early drinks might cause strong effects, but with each sip, you feel less impact.

These different forms of tolerance can fool a person into thinking they can handle more. In reality, the body is under strain, even if a person does not appear extremely drunk.

2.16 Why Quitting Can Be Hard from a Chemical Point of View

Once the body adjusts to regular alcohol intake, the internal systems expect it to be there. Suddenly removing alcohol can feel like a shock. Brain cells might fire too rapidly, causing anxiety or shaking. The nervous system might go from calm to overactive in a short period. This is why medical supervision is sometimes advised for individuals with severe dependence. Professionals can provide medications or other support to lessen withdrawal symptoms.

2.17 Surprising Health Gains After Cutting Down or Stopping

While the negative effects of alcohol are clear, the positive changes from quitting can also be strong. Many individuals who stop notice:

1. **Better Sleep**: They spend more time in deep sleep, leading to more energy during the day.
2. **Clearer Skin**: Improved hydration and nutrient intake can make the skin look healthier.
3. **Improved Mood**: The brain can recalibrate its chemicals, leading to reduced anxiety or sadness.
4. **Steadier Weight**: Without extra empty calories, some lose weight or feel more comfortable in their bodies.
5. **Healthier Liver**: If damage has not reached the severe stage, the liver may repair itself.

These changes can happen within weeks or months, depending on the individual. Even those who have been heavy drinkers for years can see big gains if they stop and give their body time to heal.

2.18 Screening Tests and Checkups

If you are considering quitting, it can be helpful to get a complete health checkup. Certain tests can show the extent of any damage:

1. **Liver Function Tests**: These blood tests measure enzymes that indicate how well the liver is working.
2. **Complete Blood Count**: Can show if there are changes in red or white blood cells often linked to heavy drinking.
3. **Imaging**: Ultrasounds or scans might show if there is scarring or inflammation in the liver or pancreas.
4. **Mental Health Evaluation**: A psychologist or psychiatrist can check if there is sadness, anxiety, or other conditions that need attention.

These tests provide a baseline. If you decide to stop, you can track improvements over time. Many find motivation in seeing how their numbers improve and how their body recovers.

2.19 Ways to Support the Body During Quitting

Cutting down or stopping can be a shock to the body. There are safe methods to reduce the impact:

1. **Stay Hydrated**: Water helps flush toxins from the system. Dehydration can worsen withdrawal symptoms.
2. **Nutrient-Dense Foods**: Eat fruits, vegetables, lean proteins, and whole grains. This supports energy levels and helps the body heal.
3. **Gentle Exercise**: Light walks or simple stretches can improve circulation and mood. Too much activity too soon can be draining, so it is wise to start slow.
4. **Check Medications**: Under professional care, some people use short-term medications to ease withdrawal. Others might need vitamins or supplements to correct deficiencies.

CHAPTER 3: REAL REASONS BEHIND PROBLEM DRINKING

In the earlier chapters, we examined the definition of problem drinking and the physical effects that come with it. We touched on some root causes, but this chapter will look more deeply into why people turn to alcohol in the first place. It will focus on the less obvious reasons, the emotional and mental elements that can drive a person toward regular heavy drinking. We will also touch on social pressures and the hidden triggers that keep this pattern going.

By the end of this chapter, you should have a clearer idea of how internal and external factors connect to create a pattern that is tough to break. You will see how stress, relationships, personal doubts, and even events from the past can play a role. Understanding these reasons can be a key part of building a better plan to stop.

3.1 Hidden Emotional Wounds

Many individuals who drink regularly are trying to numb something. That something might be guilt, sadness, memories of difficult times, or simply the stress of everyday life. When emotional scars are not addressed, the mind searches for relief. Alcohol can appear to provide a shortcut. A few drinks might reduce tension or silence certain worries, but this relief is temporary. Once the effects wear off, the emotional weight often returns heavier than before.

- **Childhood Events**: Experiences during early years can shape how a person handles problems later in life. If someone grew up in a harsh environment, they may find it difficult to manage stress in a healthy manner. Alcohol might become a way to block out painful memories or anxiety.
- **Unresolved Anger**: Some people carry anger related to family conflicts or personal disappointments. They might drink to cope with these feelings, especially if they do not have an outlet for expressing them. Over time, this pattern can become a habit.
- **Low Self-Worth**: If a person feels undeserving or has persistent self-doubt, they may turn to alcohol to feel more confident or to drown out negative self-talk.

Why It Matters

When a person realizes that heavy drinking is a reaction to emotional pain, they can begin to explore alternatives. Instead of using alcohol to reduce pain, they might consider therapy or other methods. This awareness can transform how one views their own drinking habit.

3.2 Stress and Overload

Modern life often involves juggling many tasks. Work deadlines, money issues, caring for loved ones, or dealing with health problems can increase tension. Some find it hard to cope without some kind of relief. While healthy ways of coping exist, alcohol is a quick fix that seems to require minimal effort.

- **Work Stress**: A busy schedule or a high-pressure job can push a person to seek fast relaxation. A few drinks after work can become a daily pattern. Over time, it may grow into dependence.
- **Relationship Tension**: Arguments or problems at home can lead people to drink as a way to calm themselves or avoid facing the situation. This can form a loop where alcohol leads to more arguments, which triggers further drinking.
- **Financial Concerns**: Money trouble can keep a person up at night. A bottle might feel like a quick way to quiet those worries. Yet the cost of alcohol can actually make money issues worse.

Stress that is not handled in a healthy way can make someone feel trapped. If alcohol has become a go-to response, changing that pattern can feel overwhelming. But knowing that stress is a major factor can be a sign that stress management strategies need to be part of the plan.

3.3 Social Pressure and Cultural Factors

In some circles, regular or heavy drinking might be seen as normal. Whether it is a weekly gathering at the bar or a constant stream of parties, social surroundings can lead people to think that daily drinking is acceptable. Cultural norms might add to this. Some families might serve alcohol at every meal or event, making it seem like a normal part of life.

- **Peer Approval**: Friends might tease someone who does not join in. This can cause a sense of exclusion, which can push a person to drink just to fit in.
- **Traditions**: Certain traditions revolve around alcoholic drinks. While it might be fine to participate in moderation, a pattern of heavy drinking can build up.
- **Group Dynamics**: If an entire group bonds over drinking, it can be tough for a single person to break away. Fear of missing out can keep someone stuck in a harmful pattern.

Realizing how social settings and cultural norms affect behavior can make it easier to find strategies to handle these situations without always relying on alcohol.

3.4 Learned Behavior from Family

In some cases, people pick up alcohol-related behaviors from relatives. If a parent or older sibling drank heavily, a child may grow up viewing that as normal. This can plant the seed for problem drinking later.

- **Modeling**: Children often learn by watching. If a parent deals with stress by drinking, the child might follow that method as an adult.
- **Family Secrets**: Some families keep silent about alcohol misuse, pretending everything is normal. This secrecy can add confusion for a child, who might sense that something is not right but has no explanation.
- **Inherited Traits**: While genes do not force a person to drink, certain traits linked to anxiety or impulsive behavior can be passed down. These traits might make a person more likely to form habits related to alcohol.

Not everyone who grows up around heavy drinking becomes dependent. However, seeing parents or guardians drink too much can certainly shape attitudes toward alcohol.

3.5 Personality Characteristics and Coping Styles

Each person reacts differently to stress. Some individuals might be more prone to worry or gloominess. Others might have difficulty handling anger. Alcohol misuse can be linked to how a person handles challenges:

- **Impulsiveness**: People who act on urge or emotion might be quick to grab a drink when stress hits. This can turn into a habit.
- **Need for Instant Relief**: Some prefer quick solutions instead of dealing with long-term methods like therapy. Alcohol can feel like a fast fix, even though it does not solve the root problem.
- **Seeking Thrills**: Certain people love excitement or risk. Heavy drinking can be part of that lifestyle. It might start as a social activity but become a regular pattern.

Understanding personal tendencies can help in choosing a better method of coping. A person prone to worry might benefit from structured methods like breathing exercises. An impulsive person might learn to pause before acting, using tactics to slow down decision-making.

3.6 Mental Health Factors

When a person has an underlying mental health concern like anxiety, sadness, or a panic disorder, they might lean on alcohol to lessen the emotional load. Sometimes, these conditions go undiagnosed. The individual might not even know they have a problem beyond the drinking.

- **Anxiety**: People with high anxiety might drink to calm their nerves in social settings or before tough tasks. Over time, they become reliant on alcohol to face daily events.
- **Sadness**: Alcohol can seem to lift mood for a brief period. However, it often leads to an emotional crash later. This up-and-down pattern can make sadness worse in the long run.
- **Post-Traumatic Stress**: Individuals with severe past events might use alcohol to block out upsetting memories or nightmares. This can lead to a cycle that is tough to break.

Dealing with these conditions at their source often requires professional support. If a person tries to quit drinking without addressing these deeper issues, they may find the cravings persist because the emotional needs remain unmet.

3.7 Lack of Other Outlets

Some people do not have hobbies, interests, or a strong social support group. They may feel they have nowhere else to turn when life gets hard. Alcohol becomes the one escape they can rely on.

- **Boredom**: Without regular interests, a person might fill their free time with drinks. This can slowly grow into a daily pattern.
- **Isolation**: If someone has few friends or a limited social life, drinking might feel like a companion. They might drink alone at home most nights.
- **No Healthy Stress Relief**: Activities like exercise, art, or community work can lower stress. If these do not exist in a person's life, alcohol might become the only outlet.

Recognizing boredom or loneliness as factors can be a wake-up call to develop interests or seek social connections. Finding a new activity can shift attention away from drinking.

3.8 Patterns That Form Over Time

Sometimes, there is no single event that triggers heavy drinking. Instead, multiple small factors stack up. A person might start with social drinking, then discover it also helps them relax after work. Later, they add a drink in the morning for a bit of relief before a stressful day. Over weeks or months, these little habits merge into one large pattern of dependence.

- **Habits Grow Gradually**: At first, one might not notice how often they are pouring a drink. They might think it is still under control because they are not getting arrested or passing out every night.
- **Routine Behaviors**: Drinking can become linked to certain daily rituals, like turning on the TV or eating dinner. This link is powerful because the mind begins to expect alcohol during those activities.
- **Unconscious Triggers**: The smell of a certain food or the sight of a favorite bar can spark a craving. These triggers might not be obvious unless you pay close attention.

This gradual development is why many find it hard to pinpoint the start of their problem. It sneaks up bit by bit.

3.9 Underestimating the Risks

Another reason people keep drinking heavily is that they do not see the harm. They might know alcohol can cause problems, but they think those problems happen only to others or in extreme cases.

- **Thinking You're Different**: A person might believe they are immune to the health effects. They might say, "My uncle drank for years and lived a long life." Such examples can blind them to their own risk.
- **Downplaying Physical Warnings**: Maybe they notice slight headaches or a shaky feeling in the morning, but they blame it on lack of sleep rather than alcohol.
- **Skipping Doctor Visits**: Some avoid medical checkups because they do not want to face the possibility of being told to stop drinking. This allows them to keep ignoring potential harm.

Recognizing the reality of risk can be unpleasant, but it can also motivate change before major health or relationship crises happen.

3.10 Seeking Group Acceptance

Many people fear being alone or feeling left out. If their main friend group revolves around bars or house parties, it can be hard to quit or reduce drinking. There is a fear that they will lose their social circle, which might be the only circle they have.

- **Feeling of Belonging**: Alcohol can act like a common thread among friends. Skipping drinks can lead to questions or teasing.
- **Fear of Abandonment**: A person might think, "If I stop, who will I hang out with?" This fear can keep someone stuck in a pattern even when they know it is harmful.
- **Group Identity**: In some social groups, heavy drinking might be tied to status or popularity. Going against that norm can feel uncomfortable.

Being aware of these social factors is key. It might be necessary to find new friends or activities, which can feel difficult but is often worth it for long-term health.

3.11 Advertising and Media Influence

Modern ads and movies often show alcohol as a harmless way to have fun. Characters on television might drink all day without facing real consequences. This can build the idea that heavy drinking is normal or even desirable.

- **Constant Exposure**: Billboards, online banners, and TV commercials can be everywhere. This can keep alcohol on a person's mind.

- **Subtle Pressure**: Ads might suggest you need a specific brand of alcohol to enjoy life or reduce stress. Some ads go as far as linking the drink to good looks or success.
- **Lack of Counterbalance**: While there are anti-drunk-driving ads, the overall message from mainstream media often paints drinking as glamorous. You rarely see realistic portrayals of the harm it can cause.

Recognizing the effect of media can help a person step back and think critically about what is being promoted and why.

3.12 "All or Nothing" Thinking

Some people have rigid thoughts about their own drinking. They might think they either have to keep drinking the way they do or completely lose the support of friends. This black-and-white way of seeing the world can prevent them from realizing they have options. They might feel stuck, telling themselves, "I cannot imagine life without alcohol, so I might as well keep going."

- **Fear of Failure**: If someone tries to cut down and slips up, they might see it as total failure. This can lead them to return to heavy drinking, feeling they are not capable of change.
- **Perfectionism**: A perfectionist might expect instant success in quitting. When they face any challenge, they spiral back into harmful habits.
- **Viewing Alcohol as the Only Reward**: If a person sees alcohol as their single source of enjoyment, they might fear that stopping means no joy at all.

To break from this thinking, it can help to list small steps and other rewards that do not involve alcohol. Accepting that setbacks might happen can soften that rigid mindset.

3.13 Emotional Triggers That Spark Drinking

Emotional triggers can be subtle or obvious. Many times, these triggers are linked to past events or mental habits. Common triggers include:

- **Loneliness**: Feeling alone on a weekend might lead to a bottle for company.

- **Anniversary of a Sad Event**: An approaching date linked to a painful memory can cause someone to reach for a drink to block out those thoughts.
- **Anger or Disappointment**: A fight with a spouse, a critique at work, or a personal failure can all ignite an urge to drink.

Identifying triggers in daily life is an important step toward breaking their power. Writing them down or talking them out in therapy can help a person see a pattern they never noticed.

3.14 Craving Instant Comfort

For many, the main appeal of alcohol is quick comfort. A sip might bring calm or confidence within minutes. Most positive long-term strategies, like exercise or counseling, require time and effort. The fast effect of alcohol can be very tempting by comparison.

- **Short-Term Mindset**: Some cannot think beyond the present moment. They want relief right now, and they will worry about the consequences later.
- **Escape from Boredom**: Some are not necessarily sad or anxious; they are simply bored. Alcohol offers a quick change in feeling.
- **Easing Physical Discomfort**: Some feel bodily pains that might go away or seem less intense with a few drinks. Rather than seeking medical help, they might turn to alcohol as a cheap alternative.

These aspects highlight the allure of alcohol as a fast solution. Recognizing that it is not a true fix can help shift a person's perspective.

3.15 Fear of Facing Problems Without Alcohol

Many worry that without alcohol, they will have to face inner struggles, painful memories, or current relationship issues head-on. This can be frightening. Alcohol acts like a barrier or a screen.

- **Avoidance**: Instead of addressing problems, a person might drink to numb themselves. This can stop personal growth.
- **Loss of Confidence**: Some have drunk for so long that they doubt they can cope with stress on their own. Quitting might feel like stepping into the unknown.

- **Worry About Emotions**: There is fear that sadness, guilt, or anger could be overwhelming if not kept in check by alcohol.

Facing these problems often requires courage and, in some cases, professional guidance. But it is the only real path to lasting improvement.

3.16 Influence of Other Substances

It is not unusual for people to combine alcohol with other substances. This can happen with cigarettes, prescription meds, or illicit drugs. The presence of these substances can keep the person stuck in an overall harmful pattern.

- **Nicotine and Alcohol**: Smoking and drinking are often paired. If a person tries to quit smoking, they might feel the urge to drink more, or vice versa.
- **Medication Misuse**: Some take extra pills and wash them down with alcohol to intensify effects. This is risky and can deepen the body's dependence on multiple substances.
- **Illegal Drugs**: A pattern of drug use can make it harder to reduce or stop drinking. One substance might trigger a craving for another.

Addressing multiple substances together is often crucial, because focusing on just one might leave another problem unchecked.

3.17 Past Attempts to Quit and Disappointments

Many who struggle with alcohol have tried to stop before. They might have used willpower alone, or tried a support group, only to slip back. These experiences can create a belief that change is impossible.

- **Feelings of Shame**: A failed attempt can leave a person feeling weaker or more hopeless than before.
- **Unrealistic Methods**: Some might have chosen methods that do not address the deeper causes. When that fails, they assume nothing will work.
- **Not Seeking Support**: Trying to quit alone can be tough. Without a support system, it can be easy to give up at the first sign of difficulty.

Seeing past attempts not as final failures, but as learning experiences, can be a game-changer. Each attempt might reveal a clue about what went right or wrong.

3.18 Control Issues and Rebellion

Sometimes drinking ties into control. An individual might use drinking as a way to rebel against rules or expectations. This often happens in teenagers or young adults, but can extend into adulthood.

- **Defiance**: If a person feels that family or society is imposing too many rules, they might drink heavily to prove they have free will.
- **Self-Punishment**: Some drink because they feel they do not deserve happiness, so they punish themselves in a slow, harmful way.
- **Mistaken Freedom**: A person might see heavy drinking as a sign of independence, not realizing they are becoming dependent on alcohol.

Recognizing that heavy drinking can be a form of rebellion might open the door to finding healthier ways to stand up for personal rights or express frustration.

3.19 Lack of Factual Knowledge

Although many are aware that alcohol can be harmful, few actually understand the detailed effects on the brain and body. This lack of knowledge can lead a person to continue drinking heavily, believing they can handle it.

- **Believing Myths**: Some hold onto ideas like, "Beer is safer than liquor," or, "Wine cannot hurt you because it's natural." These myths can enable heavy use.
- **Ignoring Long-Term Impact**: Without knowing the real dangers of prolonged drinking, a person might take risks they would avoid if they had full information.
- **Poor Advice**: Friends might offer incorrect guidance. For instance, someone might say, "Just drink more water," or "Eat something first," as if that will protect them from dependence.

Once a person gains accurate details, they might realize their habit is not as harmless as they once thought.

CHAPTER 4: SETTING CLEAR GOALS FOR CHANGE

Knowing the deeper reasons behind drinking sets the stage, but it is not enough on its own. To reduce or quit alcohol, it helps to form well-defined goals. A general wish like "I want to drink less" can be too vague, leaving room for excuses and slips. Clear objectives keep you focused and measure progress in a visible way. This chapter will explore how to decide your long-term and short-term goals, evaluate your relationship with alcohol, and pick a path that fits your health and personal needs.

4.1 Why Goals Matter

Goals give direction. Instead of wandering through each day hoping not to drink too much, you can aim for a specific outcome. When the mind has a target, it becomes easier to keep on track. Goals also help you see your successes, which is critical for motivation. If you have a certain number of sober days per week as a goal, you can count them and celebrate that achievement in a simple way.

- **Accountability**: Clearly stated targets can be shared with a friend, relative, or professional. This means you are not the only one monitoring your progress.
- **Reduced Ambiguity**: Vague intentions often lead to confusion. One day you might allow two drinks, another day you might let it slide to four, because there is no strict plan.
- **Steady Improvement**: Goals can be broken down into steps, making it simpler to advance without feeling overwhelmed.

4.2 Deciding Between Cutting Down and Quitting Completely

The first major decision is whether to aim for total abstinence or just drink in moderation. Different people have different needs, and this is a personal choice based on multiple factors.

1. **Health Status**: If you have a medical condition (like liver disease), your doctor might advise total abstinence. Even small amounts might harm you.

2. **Severity of Dependence**: If you experience severe withdrawal or cannot keep your intake below a certain level, quitting completely could be the safest route.
3. **Personal Preference**: Some find the concept of "one or two drinks" too tempting. For them, having zero drinks might be simpler than trying to stick to a limit.
4. **Lifestyle Factors**: If your main social group involves constant heavy drinking, moderation can be very difficult to maintain.

There is no one-size-fits-all approach. It helps to weigh the pros and cons for your specific life. Sometimes, a trial period of no drinking can show you how it feels to be alcohol-free. You can decide later if reintroducing small amounts is manageable or not.

4.3 Setting SMART Goals

A helpful approach is to set SMART goals: Specific, Measurable, Achievable, Relevant, and Time-bound. This method keeps your target clear and easier to track.

- **Specific**: "I will not drink Monday through Friday" is more precise than "I will drink less."
- **Measurable**: "I will limit my drinking to 2 standard drinks on Saturday" can be counted and tracked.
- **Achievable**: If you have been drinking every day, aiming for zero drinks all at once might be too large a jump. Instead, you might aim to cut back step by step, unless medical advice says otherwise.
- **Relevant**: Pick goals that matter to you. If your top concern is health, center your goals around health checkpoints like better sleep or improved liver tests.
- **Time-bound**: Set a clear timeline, such as "For the next 4 weeks, I will only drink on Saturday nights, and never more than 2 drinks."

Using SMART goals takes away some of the guesswork. You know exactly what you are aiming for and when you want to achieve it.

4.4 Writing Goals Down

Putting goals on paper can make them feel real. Whether it is a notebook, a phone app, or a chart on your fridge, seeing your targets in writing can strengthen your commitment.

- **Daily Reminders**: Place a note in a place you look at often, like the bathroom mirror. It keeps your goals visible and fresh in your mind.
- **Progress Tracking**: You can mark each day you meet your goal or note any slip-ups. Over time, you can see patterns and measure growth.
- **Personal Contract**: Some people sign a "contract" with themselves, stating their goals. This adds a sense of seriousness.

Seeing your goals in black and white can also help you reflect on whether they are realistic or if they need adjusting.

4.5 Breaking Down Long-Term Targets

If your ultimate aim is to quit entirely, you might divide it into smaller steps to avoid feeling overwhelmed:

- **Step 1**: Reduce drinking days from 7 per week to 5.
- **Step 2**: Keep the number of drinks per day to a certain limit.
- **Step 3**: Identify triggers and develop strategies to deal with them.
- **Step 4**: Aim for 2 alcohol-free weeks.
- **Step 5**: Move to a full month without drinking.

Each step builds on the last. This makes the overall target more achievable.

4.6 Understanding Your Motivation

Goals are more powerful when you connect them to personal reasons that matter to you. If the motivation is just to please someone else, it can be harder to stay driven. Think about why you really want to cut down or quit:

- **Health**: Maybe you want to reduce the risk of high blood pressure or other issues.

- **Family**: You might want to be more present for children or improve your marriage.
- **Financial**: Drinking can drain money that could go toward savings or other needs.
- **Personal Growth**: You might feel that alcohol is holding you back from your full potential.

List these reasons in a place you can read them daily. Knowing your "why" can keep you pushing forward when you face a craving or social pressure.

4.7 Goal Examples

Below are some sample goals, showing how they can be specific and measurable:

1. "I will not drink Monday through Thursday, and I will only have up to 2 standard drinks total on Friday and Saturday."
2. "I will track each drink in a notebook and not exceed 10 drinks total each week."
3. "I will go to a support meeting every Wednesday evening and talk to a counselor once a month for the next 3 months."
4. "I will replace my evening drink with a non-alcoholic beverage and a 30-minute walk for the next 2 weeks."

These examples show various approaches, from limiting drinks on certain days to focusing on healthier activities.

4.8 Goal Adjustments

Your goals might need to be adjusted over time. You could discover that a target is too strict, making you feel defeated if you have a slip. Or you might find you are ready for a bigger challenge. Regularly check your progress and see if changes are necessary:

- **Reduce or Increase Limits**: If you have succeeded in not drinking on weekdays, maybe you can extend that to weekends. If it is too difficult, perhaps keep one day for moderate drinking and remain alcohol-free on other days.

- **Shorten or Extend Timelines**: If a 30-day plan is too large a jump, aim for 14 days at first. If 14 days is easy, extend to 30.
- **Add New Goals**: Once you control your drinking, you might want to focus on other areas like exercise, cooking healthy meals, or improving work performance.

Goals should be flexible enough to adapt to real life, but firm enough to provide structure.

4.9 Planning for Setbacks

Nobody is perfect, and slip-ups can happen. Instead of viewing them as total failure, see them as opportunities to learn. This is a part of the process.

- **Identify Warning Signs**: Before a slip occurs, you may notice you are feeling lonely, stressed, or overly confident ("I can handle one drink"). Understanding these signals can help you take action sooner.
- **Have an Emergency Plan**: Write down what you will do if you feel an urge to drink. It could be calling a friend, leaving a certain location, or switching to a non-alcoholic beverage.
- **Review and Adjust**: If a slip happens, ask yourself what led up to it. Were you in a situation you had not planned for? Did you skip meals? Use the answers to improve your strategy.

Viewing slip-ups as data rather than disaster can keep you on track toward your ultimate goal.

4.10 Building a Support Network

While personal determination is vital, having supportive people around you can make a big difference. This can include friends, family, support groups, or online communities.

- **Choosing the Right People**: Look for individuals who respect your goals. Steer clear of those who pressure you to drink.
- **Professional Help**: Therapists or counselors can guide you through emotional concerns. Medical professionals can advise on health aspects.

- **Groups and Meetings**: There are many alcohol support programs. If meeting in person feels uncomfortable, you can find online sessions or forums.

This network can offer advice, encouragement, and a sense of shared experience. When you feel discouraged, a simple phone call or message can remind you why you set these goals in the first place.

4.11 Practical Tools for Tracking Goals

You can use several methods to keep an eye on progress:

1. **Drink Counter Apps**: Some apps let you log each drink, track sober days, and even measure money saved.
2. **Physical Calendar**: Mark off alcohol-free days with a big X. Visually seeing multiple X's in a row can feel motivating.
3. **Habit Trackers**: You can find printable trackers or use bullet journals. Write down each goal and color in a box for each day you stick to it.

Tracking can turn an abstract process into something you can see and measure daily. It also shows where you might be struggling, so you can make changes.

4.12 Setting Up Rewards and Positive Reinforcement

Rewards can be a strong motivator. When you achieve a target (like a week of staying within your limit or avoiding alcohol entirely), give yourself something you enjoy.

- **Non-Food Rewards**: Instead of using sweets or other items that might form another habit, think of small treats like new books, music, or a trip to a museum.
- **Saving Money**: If you were spending a certain amount on alcohol, put that aside in a special account or jar. Over weeks or months, you might have enough for a larger treat, like a short vacation or a purchase you have always wanted.
- **Public Acknowledgment**: Some people like to share milestones with supportive friends or online groups. Hearing "good job" can boost morale.

Rewards highlight the positive side of achieving goals, which can help you stay excited about the process.

4.13 Visualizing Success

Some find it helpful to picture themselves after reaching their goal. This is not about using fancy language or imagination to "transform" your life instantly. Rather, it is a simple exercise:

- **Detailed Picture**: Imagine what your typical day would look like if you drank less or not at all. Picture waking up feeling clear-headed, going through your routine without stress, and handling problems calmly.
- **Emotion Check**: Notice how it would feel to have fewer regrets or less guilt about drinking. Consider how your relationships might improve.
- **Practical Steps**: Tie the visualization to real steps. If you imagine yourself working out in the mornings, plan for that specifically.

This process helps keep you focused on the end result, which can strengthen your desire to follow through.

4.14 Handling Peer Pressure in Goal Setting

When you set goals, there might be people who do not respect them. They might tease you or say, "A couple of drinks won't hurt." Having a plan for these situations is key.

- **Polite Decline**: Practice a simple answer: "No thanks, I'm good," or "I'm driving tonight." It can help to have a few quick responses ready.
- **Suggest Alternatives**: If your friends always meet at a bar, propose a coffee shop, a movie, or a sports activity instead.
- **Avoiding Triggers**: If certain events always lead to heavy drinking, consider skipping them until you feel stronger in your new habits.

Sometimes, those around you might need time to adjust to the "new you." Being firm but polite can protect your progress.

4.15 Goal Setting for Physical and Mental Health

While focusing on alcohol, do not forget goals related to your overall well-being. These can reinforce each other:

- **Exercise Targets**: This might be as simple as walking 20 minutes a day, three times a week. Exercise can reduce stress and cravings.
- **Sleep Goals**: Aim for a consistent bedtime and wake time. Good rest supports mood and energy.
- **Nutritional Goals**: Plan balanced meals or consider talking to a nutrition expert. Proper nutrition can help with withdrawal and improve how you feel day to day.

Setting these health-related goals can boost your sense of control and reinforce your progress in cutting down on alcohol.

4.16 Using "If-Then" Plans

An "if-then" plan is a clear statement of what you will do if a certain situation arises. This helps you respond quickly instead of caving to impulse.

- **Example 1**: "If my friend invites me for a night out, then I will drive myself so I can leave early if I feel pressured to drink."
- **Example 2**: "If I start to feel upset after work, then I will go for a short walk instead of having a drink."
- **Example 3**: "If I find myself at home alone on a weekend, then I will watch a comedy show or listen to upbeat music to shift my mood."

These plans remove guesswork. Instead of deciding in the heat of the moment, you have a script to follow.

4.17 Handling Other People's Expectations

You might face pushback from people who have seen you as a drinker for a long time. They might say, "You used to be fun," or "One drink won't kill you." It is crucial to handle these comments without giving in.

- **Calm Explanations**: You can say, "I'm focusing on my health right now," or "I'm taking a break from alcohol to meet some personal goals." You do not owe anyone a lengthy explanation.

- **Firm Boundaries**: If someone persists, repeat your stance. If they continue, consider stepping away from the conversation or the event.
- **Positive Replacements**: Show them that you can still have fun without drinking. Participate in group activities that do not revolve around alcohol.

Sticking to your goals in social situations can be one of the biggest challenges, but it also strengthens your resolve and shows others you are serious.

4.18 Measuring Success Beyond Just Numbers

Counting drinks or sober days is useful, but there are other ways to see progress:

- **Mood Improvements**: Note if you feel calmer, happier, or less anxious.
- **Physical Changes**: Better sleep, less bloating, and more energy can be big wins.
- **Social Interactions**: Maybe you are having better conversations with loved ones or feeling more present.
- **Self-Esteem**: Notice if you feel proud of yourself more often. This self-confidence can be a strong sign of progress.

Sometimes, these changes happen before the numbers drastically drop. Observing them can keep you inspired to continue.

4.19 Knowing When to Seek Professional Guidance

While goal setting can be done on your own, some situations call for expert help:

- **Severe Dependence**: If you have intense withdrawal symptoms (like shaking, sweating, or seizures), it is wise to consult a medical professional.
- **Co-Existing Conditions**: If you suspect you have sadness, anxiety, or another mental health issue, a counselor or psychiatrist can help you address both alcohol use and these conditions at the same time.
- **Repeated Failed Attempts**: If you have tried many times without success, a more structured program might be necessary. This could include therapy, medication, or specialized treatment groups.

Seeking help is not a sign of weakness. It is often the smartest step toward lasting success.

CHAPTER 5: PLANNING AND PREPARING FOR A BETTER FUTURE

In the last chapter, we discussed the importance of setting clear goals for cutting down or stopping alcohol use. Goals give you a direction and help you measure progress. Now, it is time to focus on the practical steps needed to move from talking about change to actually making it happen. This chapter will explore how to organize your home, routines, finances, and social life in a way that supports your plan. We will also look at ways to handle early doubts and hesitations. By the end, you should have a framework for preparing a stable path toward an alcohol-free life.

5.1 Why Planning Matters

People sometimes think they can just stop drinking once they make up their mind. But daily life has a way of throwing challenges at you. A good plan helps you deal with triggers, stress, and unexpected events without returning to harmful patterns. It sets up a structure that reduces uncertainty and provides a sense of control.

- **Strong Foundation**: Without preparation, a person may give in at the first sign of stress. Good planning can prevent setbacks.
- **Confidence**: When you have a to-do list or clear steps, you are less likely to feel overwhelmed. You can remind yourself, "I have a strategy for that."
- **Long-Range Focus**: Planning is not just for the short term. It also shows how you can maintain positive habits for months or years.

5.2 Organizing Your Living Space

Your home should be a safe zone as you work on your alcohol goals. If your place is filled with reminders of drinking, it can be tough to avoid thinking about it. Here are some practical tips:

1. **Remove Visible Triggers**: This includes empty bottles, barware, and any decorations or ads that remind you of drinking. You do not need to toss everything if you have shared living arrangements, but consider storing these items out of sight.

2. **Create a Calm Space**: If you have a spot where you used to drink, convert it into a reading corner or a place for a new activity. This helps break the mental link between that space and alcohol.
3. **Stock Up on Alternatives**: Keep a variety of non-alcoholic drinks at home. This can include flavored water, herbal tea, or fruit juices. Having options on hand makes it easier to pick something else when you are thirsty.
4. **List Important Contacts**: Keep a small list of phone numbers for friends, a counselor, or a help hotline in a visible spot. If you feel a craving building, you can call or text someone right away.

5.3 Building a Daily Routine

Unstructured time can make it easy to slip back into old habits. A routine gives you a sense of purpose and reduces boredom.

- **Morning Rituals**: Start the day with a simple habit, like drinking a glass of water, stretching, or writing in a journal. This sets a positive tone for the day.
- **Regular Meals**: Skipping meals can lead to drops in energy, which might spark cravings. Plan balanced meals at regular times.
- **Scheduled Activities**: If you used to spend evenings drinking, fill that slot with something else, such as a walk, an online course, or a hobby.
- **Wind-Down Time**: Before bed, set aside 30 minutes for low-stress activities like reading, mild stretching, or listening to soothing music. This can improve sleep quality.

Having a daily routine does not mean you lose freedom. It means you choose in advance how you will use your time, leaving less room for harmful impulses.

5.4 Arranging Your Finances

Alcohol can be expensive. Many people find they save a surprising amount of money once they cut back or stop. Taking control of your finances can also reduce stress.

1. **Track Spending**: Write down how much you spend on alcohol in a typical week or month. The total might motivate you to stay on track once you see the potential savings.

2. **Open a Separate Account or Jar**: Each time you skip buying drinks, move that money into a savings account or a jar. Over weeks or months, you can use these funds for something meaningful, like a home improvement or a class you always wanted to take.
3. **Budget for New Activities**: If you want to start a new hobby (like painting, fishing, or learning a skill), plan for any costs in your budget. Using money you no longer spend on alcohol can help you get started.
4. **Emergency Fund**: Try to build an emergency fund. This can lower financial worries, making you less likely to reach for a drink when unexpected bills or other stressors pop up.

5.5 Creating a Supportive Social Network

People can be one of the biggest influences on your behavior. Some will encourage you, while others might challenge your new choices. It is important to identify who is helpful and who is not.

- **List Trusted People**: Write down names of friends, relatives, or coworkers you trust to support your goals. You can speak to them about your plans or ask them to check in on you regularly.
- **Set Boundaries**: If there are people who pressure you to drink or tease you about not drinking, think about limiting contact until you feel more confident.
- **In-Person vs. Online Support**: Both can be helpful. Local support groups can provide face-to-face contact. Online communities can offer quick support at any hour.
- **Communicate Your Needs**: Telling your circle, "I'm planning to reduce or stop drinking, and I'd appreciate your help," can clear up misunderstandings. Some people just need to hear your reasons so they can be more supportive.

5.6 Planning for Triggers and High-Risk Situations

A trigger is anything that lights the urge to drink. High-risk situations can be social events, emotional states, or even physical locations where you used to drink regularly. It is wise to plan how you will handle them before they happen.

1. **Identify Your Top Triggers**: These might be certain friends, bars, times of day, or moods (like anger or sadness).

2. **Avoid or Alter the Situation**: If possible, stay away from the highest-risk places or events at first. If you cannot avoid them, make a plan, such as bringing a non-alcoholic drink or having a friend who also does not drink.
3. **Set a Time Limit**: If you must attend an event with alcohol, plan to leave after a certain amount of time. Knowing you have an exit strategy can reduce anxiety.
4. **Prepare Responses**: People might offer you a drink. Practice a simple reply like, "No thanks, I'm good," or, "I'm trying something new with my health." You do not have to give a long explanation.

5.7 Communicating with Family or Roommates

If you live with other people, it helps to talk about your plan. You do not want to feel tempted by alcohol in the kitchen or pressured to join in every weekend.

- **Honest Discussion**: Explain what you are aiming for. Ask them not to bring alcohol home or at least not to offer it to you.
- **Shared Responsibility**: If finances are shared, talk about how cutting back can help everyone.
- **Brainstorm Alternatives**: Instead of gatherings that revolve around alcohol, propose other activities like board games, outdoor walks, or simple get-togethers with snacks and soft drinks.
- **Ask for Patience**: Let them know you might have mood swings or stress as you adjust. Encourage them to ask how they can help, rather than guessing.

5.8 Learning from Past Attempts

Some individuals may have tried to quit or cut down before. If that describes you, consider what you can learn from those efforts. Even if you did not stick with it, you likely picked up helpful knowledge.

- **What Worked**: Maybe you found that calling a specific friend or going for a run in the evening worked well. Keep that in your plan.
- **What Went Wrong**: Think about where you felt overwhelmed. Was it social pressure, boredom, or stress? Look for ways to strengthen your approach this time.

- **Add Missing Pieces**: If you did not get medical advice in the past, consider getting it now. If you avoided support groups, maybe this time you can join one or seek an online community.

5.9 Setting Ground Rules for Yourself

Rules can help you navigate everyday situations without constant internal debates. For instance:

- **No Alcohol in the House**: If you decide to keep alcohol away, do not break that rule "just this once." That can start a slippery slope.
- **Check in with Yourself**: Before any social event, ask, "Am I likely to feel pressured to drink?" If the answer is yes, decide on a strategy or skip it entirely if you are not ready.
- **Delay Strategy**: If a craving hits, wait 15 minutes. Use that time to drink water, do some deep breathing, or call someone. Often the craving will fade.
- **Reward Yourself**: Each day or week you stick to the rules, do something you enjoy (that does not involve drinking). This might be a small purchase, a new book, or just a relaxing break.

5.10 Introducing New Hobbies and Interests

When you remove alcohol from your life, you open space for new interests. This can be a source of excitement and can give you fresh energy.

- **Try Activities You Used to Enjoy**: Maybe you once loved drawing, playing a sport, or writing. Revisiting those can bring back positive memories.
- **Explore New Skills**: You could learn a language online or take a class on woodworking, cooking, or any subject that sparks your curiosity.
- **Physical Activities**: Exercise can lift your mood and reduce cravings. It does not have to be intense. Simple walks, swimming, or group fitness classes can help your body and mind.
- **Volunteer Work**: Helping others can give a sense of purpose. It also keeps you busy in a positive setting where alcohol is typically not the focus.

5.11 Managing Anxiety About Change

It is normal to feel anxious when doing something new. Change means stepping into the unknown, which can bring nervousness.

- **Realistic Expectations**: Accept that it might take time to feel comfortable without alcohol. The first weeks or months can be tricky.
- **Relaxation Methods**: Simple breathing techniques, light stretching, or calming music can lower anxiety. You can schedule these methods into your daily routine.
- **Professional Help**: If anxiety is severe, consider talking to a counselor or doctor. There might be techniques or treatments that can help you adjust with less stress.
- **Positive Self-Talk**: Remind yourself that challenges are part of progress. Thoughts like, "I can handle this one day at a time," or, "I have overcome things before," can provide a calm sense of control.

5.12 Organizing Medical and Professional Support

If your alcohol use is heavy or if you have any medical concerns, it is wise to get a professional opinion. Even if your drinking is moderate, expert help can make the process smoother.

- **Doctor's Checkup**: Let your doctor know about your plan. They can do blood tests or check your overall health to spot any potential problems early.
- **Therapy or Counseling**: A mental health professional can help you understand your triggers, develop coping methods, and keep you accountable.
- **Support Groups**: Local or online groups can offer guidance and understanding from others who have faced similar challenges.
- **Nutritional Guidance**: Heavy drinkers sometimes have vitamin shortages. A nutrition expert can help you form a diet that improves energy and reduces cravings.

5.13 Building a Cravings Toolkit

Cravings will likely happen, especially in the early phases. Having a set of tools to handle them is crucial.

1. **Substitute Actions**: For instance, if you feel a craving around 7 p.m., that could be your time to take a short walk or do a relaxing activity.
2. **Distraction Items**: Keep items handy that can quickly engage your mind—like a puzzle book, a stress ball, or a music playlist you love.
3. **Phone a Friend**: Ask a trusted person if you can call them when you feel a craving coming on. Even a short chat can shift your thoughts.
4. **Remind Yourself of Consequences**: Think of why you decided to change. Recall health issues, money problems, or relationship stresses caused by drinking. This can cool the urge to give in.

5.14 Handling Work and Social Obligations

Work events, parties, and holidays can bring temptations. Plan in advance how you will manage them without feeling awkward.

- **Plan Your Own Transport**: If you drive yourself, you can leave when you want. This prevents being stuck in a drinking environment longer than you can handle.
- **Talk to HR or a Supervisor**: If work gatherings involve heavy drinking, you can ask if there are non-alcoholic options or if they can schedule more varied team activities.
- **Signal Early**: If someone at the office invites you for happy hour, mention you are cutting down. Sometimes, that alone reduces their pressure to offer drinks.
- **Set Limits**: If you do attend, decide on a limit (like staying one hour) and a plan for what you will drink (like club soda with lime).

5.15 Travel and Vacations

Traveling can be a common time to overindulge. You might face free drinks on flights, mini-bars in hotels, or social gatherings while away from home.

- **Book Lodgings Without a Mini-Bar**: Or ask the hotel to remove it before you arrive.
- **Bring Your Own Snacks**: Keep healthy snacks or non-alcoholic drinks to avoid being tempted by bar stops.
- **Research Activities**: Look for sightseeing, local tours, or outdoor fun instead of bars or clubs.

- **Check Local Support Options**: If you travel often, find out if there are local support groups at your destination or if you can attend online meetings during your trip.

5.16 Guarding Against Overconfidence

After a few weeks or months of success, you might feel you have everything under control. Overconfidence can lead to carelessness. You might start thinking, "I can just have one or two drinks," which can trigger a slip.

- **Stick to the Plan**: Even if you feel strong, continue your strategies. Keep following the routines, support networks, and ground rules that brought success.
- **Watch for Subtle Slips**: It might begin with small exceptions, like accepting a drink at a party or not tracking your intake. Stay alert to these small changes in behavior.
- **Continue Learning**: Read books or articles about recovery, or keep attending support groups. Knowledge can keep you cautious and mindful.

5.17 Dealing with Boredom and Free Time

One hidden danger in early recovery is having too much idle time. If you used to fill your evenings with drinks, you now have open hours that can lead to restlessness or cravings.

- **Have a List of Fun Activities**: Write down easy activities you can do right away (such as baking something new, watching an interesting documentary, starting a simple home project).
- **Try a Physical Outlet**: Light exercise or even just a walk can break the monotony. Movement also helps clear your head.
- **Self-Improvement**: Consider online courses, podcasts, or tutorials that teach practical skills or spark your interest.
- **Social Interaction**: Chat with supportive friends, join a local club (like a chess club or a cooking group), or volunteer at community events. Interaction can keep your mind active.

5.18 Building Emotional Awareness

Many individuals drink when they cannot handle certain feelings. Developing emotional awareness can lessen that urge.

- **Daily Check-In**: Spend a few minutes each day asking yourself how you feel (happy, sad, anxious, or frustrated).
- **Naming Emotions**: Simply naming an emotion, like "I feel anxious right now," can reduce its power.
- **Journaling**: Writing down thoughts and feelings can release built-up tension and help you spot patterns over time.
- **Mindful Moments**: This does not have to be complex. Even 2–3 minutes focusing on your breath or observing your surroundings can calm the mind.

5.19 Rewarding Yourself in Healthy Ways

Removing alcohol does not mean your life should lack enjoyment. You can still treat yourself and have fun.

- **Daily Small Rewards**: This could be playing a favorite song, having a comforting cup of tea, or watching a funny video clip.
- **Weekly or Monthly Treat**: Buy yourself something inexpensive but meaningful, or plan a small outing that does not revolve around drinking.
- **Celebrate Milestones**: If you reach 30 days alcohol-free (or a certain time with lowered intake), mark it with a special meal or an experience you have been wanting to try.
- **Share Achievements**: Telling a friend or a support group that you have reached a milestone can feel good. Hearing their positive feedback also helps keep you motivated.

CHAPTER 6: HANDLING WITHDRAWAL SAFELY

For many people, the toughest part of quitting or cutting back on alcohol is dealing with withdrawal. Alcohol withdrawal can be uncomfortable and, in some cases, dangerous. It involves both physical and mental symptoms that arise when your body no longer gets the substance it has grown used to. Understanding what to expect and how to respond can help you stay safe and calm during this phase.

6.1 What Is Alcohol Withdrawal?

Withdrawal occurs when the body has adapted to a substance, and that substance is suddenly reduced or removed. With alcohol, a person who drinks heavily over a long period may find that their brain and other systems depend on alcohol to function at their "new normal." Once that daily intake drops, the body reacts.

- **Physical Symptoms**: Sweating, shaking, nausea, and headaches. In more severe cases, there can be seizures or serious confusion.
- **Mental or Emotional Symptoms**: Anxiety, trouble sleeping, mood swings, or feeling extremely on edge.
- **Timing**: Symptoms can appear as early as a few hours after the last drink, or they might begin 24–48 hours later, depending on how the person's body processes alcohol.

Not everyone goes through severe withdrawal. Some might only feel mild discomfort. But if you have been drinking a lot for a long time, it is crucial to understand the warning signs.

6.2 Recognizing Different Levels of Withdrawal

Withdrawal can range from mild to life-threatening. These levels usually depend on how heavily and for how long you have been drinking, as well as personal health factors.

1. **Mild**: Tremors in the hands, difficulty sleeping, headaches, mild anxiety. People at this stage might also feel queasy or sweaty, but generally stay oriented and able to function.

2. **Moderate**: Symptoms intensify, with pronounced shaking, racing heartbeat, elevated blood pressure, and higher anxiety. You might also feel more agitated or confused.
3. **Severe**: This is sometimes called delirium tremens (DTs). It can include fever, severe confusion, hallucinations (seeing or hearing things that are not there), and seizures. This level can be fatal if not treated properly.

6.3 Medical Risks and Warning Signs

Some individuals at high risk for serious withdrawal include those who have a long history of heavy drinking, past withdrawal complications, or health conditions like heart problems or liver disease. Warning signs that require immediate attention:

- **Severe Confusion or Disorientation**
- **Hallucinations** (visual or auditory)
- **Seizures** (body jerks or stiffening unexpectedly)
- **Fever or Profound Sweating**
- **Rapid Heartbeat that Feels Unmanageable**

If you or someone around you experiences these signs, it is important to get medical help as soon as possible.

6.4 Preparing for Withdrawal in Advance

If you know you will be cutting back or stopping, it can help to prepare. This reduces panic if symptoms appear.

- **Medical Check**: Talk to a doctor before making big changes, especially if you have been a heavy drinker for an extended period. They might suggest a tapering plan (gradually reducing alcohol) instead of quitting all at once.
- **Support Person**: Ask a friend or family member to be available to check on you. They can help you get medical care if needed.
- **Hydration and Nutrition**: Stock up on water, electrolyte drinks, and easy-to-digest foods. During withdrawal, your appetite might drop, so have mild foods like soups or crackers.

- **Comfort Items**: Think about what helps you stay calm—perhaps a soft blanket, some calm music, or a favorite show. Being prepared can make the process less stressful.

6.5 Safe Tapering Methods

Tapering means cutting back slowly, so the body has time to adjust. This might help reduce the intensity of symptoms. Note that if you are severely dependent, tapering at home can still be risky. You might need medical oversight.

- **Set a Daily Limit**: For instance, if you usually have 10 drinks a day, you might reduce to 8, then 6, then 4, and so on, over a set period.
- **Regular Checks**: Monitor how you feel physically and mentally. If you notice rapid heart rate or severe shaking, talk to a health professional.
- **No Unscheduled Binges**: During tapering, avoid days of extra drinking. That defeats the purpose and can shock your system.
- **Consider Professional Guidance**: A doctor can help design a tapering schedule that matches your health and circumstances.

6.6 Medical Detox and Professional Support

If your dependence is severe, a medically supervised detox might be the safest choice. This usually happens at a treatment center or hospital. Health experts can monitor vital signs, provide IV fluids if needed, and give medications to reduce severe symptoms.

- **Medication Options**: Certain drugs can help control shaking, anxiety, or seizures. A professional will decide if these are needed.
- **Round-the-Clock Care**: Nurses or other medical staff might check your blood pressure, heart rate, and temperature. They can catch problems early.
- **Safety Net**: If complications arise (like a seizure), help is immediate. This can reduce the chance of serious harm.
- **Scheduled Activities**: Some programs also include counseling or group sessions, even during detox, to help you start building strategies for long-term change.

6.7 Common Medications for Withdrawal

If you see a doctor during withdrawal, they might talk about certain medications. These can vary, but a few common ones include:

1. **Benzodiazepines**: Drugs like diazepam or chlordiazepoxide can calm the nervous system and lower the risk of seizures.
2. **Beta-Blockers**: These reduce symptoms like trembling and racing heart, but they might not help with anxiety or seizures as effectively as benzodiazepines.
3. **Anticonvulsants**: Medicines that help prevent or control seizures.
4. **Vitamins**: Chronic drinking often depletes nutrients like thiamine (vitamin B1), which is critical for brain function. A doctor might give vitamin supplements to prevent complications.

Never start or stop medications on your own. If you are concerned about withdrawal, see a healthcare provider who can guide you.

6.8 Coping with Mild to Moderate Symptoms at Home

If your withdrawal is expected to be mild and you have medical approval to handle it at home, here are some ways to get through it:

- **Stay Hydrated**: Try to drink plenty of water or electrolyte solutions. This helps offset sweating and any digestive troubles.
- **Light Meals**: Bland foods like oatmeal, toast, or soup can be easier to handle if you are feeling nauseous.
- **Reduce Stimulation**: Loud noises or bright lights can worsen anxiety or tremors. Keeping the environment calm can help.
- **Relaxation Methods**: Simple breathing exercises, listening to soothing music, or taking a warm bath can ease tension.
- **Stay Connected**: Let a trusted friend or family member know you are going through withdrawal. Ask them to check in on you regularly.

6.9 Handling Anxiety and Insomnia

Anxiety and insomnia are common in withdrawal. Not being able to sleep can make your mind race, increasing the urge to drink for relief.

1. **Limit Caffeine**: Coffee or soda can worsen anxiety and disrupt sleep. Try herbal tea or decaf drinks instead.
2. **Bedroom Routine**: Keep your bedroom dark, quiet, and cool. Turn off screens 30 minutes before bed to help your mind settle.
3. **Breathing Exercises**: Slowly inhale for a count of four, hold for a second, then exhale for a count of four. Repeat until you feel calmer.
4. **Writing It Down**: If worries keep you awake, write them on a notepad. Promise yourself you will look at them in the morning. This can sometimes quiet your mind.

6.10 Changes in Appetite and Cravings for Sugar

When you stop drinking, you might notice intense sugar cravings. Alcohol is high in calories and sugar, so your body may seek a replacement. Some suggestions:

- **Healthier Snacks**: Instead of candy, try whole fruit, yogurt with berries, or a small handful of nuts.
- **Balance Your Meals**: Ensure you get protein, healthy fats, and complex carbs. This can reduce sudden sugar urges.
- **Check for Hidden Sugars**: Sports drinks or fruit juices can also be high in sugar. Limit these if you notice you feel jittery after drinking them.
- **Gradual Reduction**: If you find yourself reaching for sweets too often, gradually reduce the portion size rather than stopping all at once. Sudden changes can trigger strong cravings.

6.11 Emotional Swings and Irritability

Your mood might be all over the place during withdrawal. It is part of the body recalibrating itself after being used to alcohol's effects.

- **Acknowledge Feelings**: It is normal to feel angry, sad, or jumpy. Telling yourself, "This is part of the process," can help you stay calm.
- **Talk It Out**: If possible, chat with a friend, support group, or counselor. Verbalizing emotions can relieve some pressure.
- **Physical Outlets**: A quick walk or simple exercise at home can burn off nervous energy. It also releases endorphins that improve mood.
- **Avoid Major Decisions**: Try not to make life-altering choices (like quitting your job or moving) in the middle of withdrawal. Wait until your mind is clearer.

6.12 Dealing with Seizure Risk

One of the most serious withdrawal complications is the risk of seizures. This risk is higher for individuals with a history of severe alcohol use or those who had seizures in past withdrawals.

- **Seek Medical Help**: If you suspect a seizure might happen or if you experience unusual shaking or confusion, contact a doctor right away.
- **Safety Measures at Home**: If possible, have someone stay with you during the first 72 hours of stopping. Make sure your environment is free of sharp edges or clutter that could be dangerous if you fall.
- **Follow Professional Advice**: If prescribed any anticonvulsant or anti-anxiety medication, take it exactly as directed.

6.13 How Long Withdrawal Can Last

Alcohol withdrawal symptoms often peak in the first 24–72 hours. Mild to moderate symptoms might start improving after a few days. However, some issues, like mood swings or sleep disturbances, can linger for weeks.

- **Acute Phase**: Usually covers the first 3–7 days, when symptoms are strongest.
- **Sub-Acute Phase**: The following 1–2 weeks, when many physical symptoms begin to settle, but emotional symptoms might continue.
- **Longer-Term Adjustments**: Some people have occasional cravings or anxiety for months, but these usually become more manageable over time.

6.14 Post-Acute Withdrawal (PAWS)

After the initial detox phase, some individuals experience post-acute withdrawal syndrome (PAWS). This can include lingering mood issues, trouble focusing, and low energy. PAWS can come in waves, improving for a while, then flaring up again.

- **Stay Informed**: Recognizing PAWS means you are not shocked when these symptoms appear.

- **Continued Support**: Ongoing therapy, support group attendance, or regular checkups with a doctor can help you manage these ups and downs.
- **Self-Care Routine**: Good sleep, balanced meals, and gentle exercise are more important than ever during PAWS.

6.15 Monitoring Heart Rate and Blood Pressure

Alcohol withdrawal can raise blood pressure and heart rate, sometimes to risky levels. If you have a blood pressure machine at home, check it regularly.

- **Alarm Threshold**: Ask your doctor what numbers are unsafe. If your blood pressure or heart rate spikes too high or stays elevated, seek guidance.
- **Relaxation Techniques**: Sitting quietly, taking slow breaths, and practicing muscle relaxation can help bring heart rate down.
- **Medication Compliance**: If you are given blood pressure medications during withdrawal, do not skip doses.

6.16 When to Return to a Health Professional

Sometimes, you might think you have passed the worst part of withdrawal, but new symptoms can appear, or existing ones might worsen.

- **Severe Headaches or Dizziness**
- **Chest Pain or Irregular Heartbeat**
- **Constant Vomiting or Diarrhea**
- **Feeling of Extreme Confusion or Panic**
- **Passing Out or Ongoing Weakness**

If you face any of these, do not hesitate to get in touch with a doctor. Delaying might lead to complications that are harder to handle later.

6.17 Using Breathing and Relaxation Tools

When anxiety spikes during withdrawal, simple breathing exercises can be surprisingly effective. For example:

1. **4-7-8 Breathing**: Breathe in for 4 seconds, hold for 7, and exhale for 8. Repeat several times.
2. **Progressive Muscle Relaxation**: Tense a group of muscles (like your shoulders), hold for a moment, then let go. Move through different parts of your body.
3. **Visualization**: Picture a calm place or memory. Focus on sensory details—what you see, hear, and feel.

These techniques might not erase withdrawal, but they can lessen panic, making it easier to cope.

6.18 Getting Emotional Support

Withdrawal can be a lonely process if you do it by yourself. Emotional support can improve your chance of success and keep you steady.

- **Friends and Family**: Trusted people can bring you food, help around the house, or just keep you company.
- **Hotlines**: Many regions have phone lines where you can talk to someone trained to support people dealing with addiction.
- **Online Forums**: If you cannot leave the house, online support groups or forums can offer immediate advice and empathy.
- **Check-Ins**: Set up times when a friend or support person calls you or visits. Knowing you have someone looking out for you can ease worry.

6.19 Planning for Post-Withdrawal Life

Getting through withdrawal is only one step. The next phase is staying alcohol-free or at a much lower intake. This requires continued effort.

- **Refine Your Triggers List**: Withdrawal might reveal new triggers you did not notice before. Update your strategies.
- **Keep a Recovery Routine**: The daily structure you built before stopping can continue. You might adjust it based on what you learned from withdrawal.
- **Focus on Other Aspects**: Once withdrawal is over, you can concentrate on building new hobbies, improving relationships, and managing stress in healthier ways.

CHAPTER 7: BUILDING A STRONG SUPPORT SYSTEM

In previous chapters, we examined how to set goals and handle withdrawal safely. These steps are important, but it is very difficult to make lasting changes without support. It is common for people to try and quit alcohol on their own. Some succeed, but many find that having the help of others makes the process smoother and more sustainable. This chapter will show you ways to build and maintain a solid support system. We will look at how to find allies in your family, friends, coworkers, and professional helpers. We will also discuss common pitfalls and how to handle people who might not respect your new choices.

7.1 The Importance of Support

Trying to quit or reduce alcohol alone can lead to feelings of isolation. When you have people who understand or at least respect your goals, you gain encouragement. They can keep you grounded when cravings rise. They can give you honest feedback and practical assistance. Having reliable support can also help with accountability. For example, if you tell your friend or spouse you plan to remain alcohol-free for the weekend, you might feel a stronger need to stick to that commitment.

Key Points:

- Encouragement: A few kind words can boost your mood when you feel weak.
- Accountability: Telling others can make it harder to slip up without noticing.
- Practical Help: People can lend a hand with chores, errands, or childcare if you are going through a tough time.

7.2 Identifying the Right People

Not everyone in your life will be an ideal support. Some might openly criticize your plan or keep pressuring you to drink "like old times." Others might mean well, but they have little understanding of the difficulties you face. Ideally, you want people who are good listeners, patient, and ready to offer help without judgment.

- **Close Friends and Family**: Consider those who have shown genuine concern for your well-being in the past.
- **Fellow Group Members**: If you attend any local or online support group, you may meet people who understand exactly what you are going through.
- **Supportive Coworkers**: Some coworkers might be encouraging if they know about your plan. They might help you skip office gatherings full of drinking or stand by you if others make comments.
- **Neighbors or Community Members**: Sometimes, the best support can come from unexpected places, like a friendly neighbor who appreciates your efforts.

Red Flag: If someone in your circle frequently makes you feel guilty or ashamed, they might not be the best source of support, at least in the early stages. It is okay to set boundaries.

7.3 Understanding Different Types of Support

There are various ways that others can help you. Some might be best at emotional support, while others are good at offering practical tips or solutions:

1. **Emotional Support**: People who listen, encourage you when you are down, and show empathy. They do not judge you for the feelings you experience.
2. **Informational Support**: Individuals who share knowledge, resources, or advice about quitting alcohol. They might recommend good treatment programs or share a helpful article.
3. **Companionship**: Those who spend time with you, engage in sober activities, and keep you company so you do not feel lonely or bored (both can lead to relapse).
4. **Accountability**: Friends or mentors who check in on your progress. They remind you of your goals and help you stay honest about your actions.

7.4 How to Ask for Help

Reaching out for support can feel awkward, especially if you are used to dealing with problems alone. However, many people are willing to help if you are clear about what you need.

- **Be Honest**: Explain that you are working to reduce or stop drinking. Let them know it is a serious effort, and you value their help.
- **Define Specific Ways to Assist**: Instead of saying "Help me," consider requests like:
    - "Can you check in on me once a week to ask how I'm doing?"
    - "Can we plan social outings that do not involve alcohol?"
    - "If you see me struggling at an event, can we leave together or talk about it privately?"
- **Pick the Right Moment**: It might not be best to have this talk during a holiday party or family reunion. Find a calm time, either in person or by phone, to discuss your plan.
- **Accept Different Reactions**: Some people might be thrilled to help, while others might be uncomfortable. That is okay; focus on those who show genuine willingness.

7.5 Friends Who Still Drink

One tricky situation is how to handle friends who still drink, especially if you used to drink together often. You do not necessarily have to cut ties with them, but you do need to be realistic about the possibility that they may continue their habits.

- **Set Boundaries**: Kindly ask that they not offer you drinks. If they keep pushing, it might be wise to limit time around them, at least until you feel stronger.
- **Suggest Alternative Activities**: If your friendship is based on going to bars, find other ways to spend time: game nights, movie nights, sports, or shared hobbies.
- **Honesty**: Let them know you value their friendship but are now focusing on your health. If they care, they should be open to changing the usual plans.

- **Plan Exits**: If you choose to attend a party with them and feel tempted, have a plan to exit. Drive yourself or arrange another way to leave when you need to.

Some friends may adjust well, while others might not. It is important to stay true to your own needs rather than trying to please everyone.

7.6 Family Dynamics

Family support can be a major asset, but it can also be complex. Some family members might have their own issues with alcohol. Others might not understand your struggles, or they might resent the extra attention you receive.

- **Clear Communication**: Explain what you are trying to do and why. Ask them to avoid bringing alcohol to family events, if possible.
- **Seek Mediation**: If conflicts arise, or if you have serious family disputes, consider seeing a family therapist. A neutral mediator can help everyone express concerns in a calm setting.
- **Balance**: You do not want to rely on just one family member for all your emotional needs. Spread out your support among different sources, so no one person feels overwhelmed.
- **Respect Boundaries**: If a family member does not want to change their own drinking habits, you might need to limit your time around them or find ways to handle visits that reduce stress.

7.7 Support Groups: In-Person and Online

Support groups offer a way to connect with individuals on a similar path. Everyone in these groups shares a common goal, so you can swap stories, lessons, and tips. Traditional in-person groups are popular and can be found in many towns. Online options are also available, and they are helpful if you have transportation issues, schedule conflicts, or simply prefer the comfort of home.

- **Local Groups**: These might be run by community organizations or churches. You can ask a doctor or counselor to recommend a group.

- **Online Forums and Meetings**: Websites and apps enable you to join discussions. Some hold live group video meetings, where people check in from different parts of the world.
- **Choosing a Format**: Some groups follow a structured program with steps, while others are more casual. Find one that matches your comfort level.
- **Benefits**: Hearing other people's experiences can help you feel less alone. You might pick up new strategies for dealing with stress or social events.

7.8 Professional Resources

Aside from support groups, many professionals can be part of your team:

1. **Therapists or Counselors**: These experts can help you work on emotional triggers, stress, and unhealthy beliefs that lead to drinking.
2. **Doctors**: A physician can guide you through withdrawal, run health checks, and prescribe medications if needed.
3. **Nutritionists**: Since alcohol misuse can impact diet, a nutritionist can help you regain balance in your food choices.
4. **Recovery Coaches**: Some individuals hire a coach to keep them focused on daily goals. Coaches can offer motivation, strategies, and accountability.

It is okay to reach out for professional help even if you do not have severe issues. Early support can prevent smaller problems from growing.

7.9 Setting Up Accountability

Accountability means you let someone else know what you are aiming for and allow them to check in on you. This helps reduce hidden slips. If you keep your plan private, it can be easy to quietly break your rules. When someone else is aware, you might pause before having that "one drink."

- **Accountability Buddy**: Choose a friend or family member who can handle the responsibility. You may agree to text each night or meet once a week.
- **Checklists**: Some people create a simple daily checklist or use a smartphone app. They mark each day they stick to the plan. They might share this chart with their accountability buddy.

- **Group Updates**: If you are in a group, you can give a brief weekly update. Just knowing others expect you to report back can give you an extra push to stay on track.

7.10 Workplace Support

Work can be a tough environment if coworkers often gather around alcohol after hours or if company events include heavy drinking. You can still find or create support at work:

- **HR or Employee Assistance**: Many workplaces have resources to help with personal issues. This might include free counseling sessions.
- **Wellness Programs**: Some companies run wellness challenges, gym memberships, or health workshops. Joining these can connect you with others who are also focusing on healthier habits.
- **Trusted Colleague**: You may have a close coworker who knows about your plan. Let them know you might need help resisting certain after-work activities.
- **Limiting Drinking Events**: If your team regularly goes out for drinks, suggest an alternative (a coffee shop or a team-building exercise). If that is not possible, set a boundary on how long you will attend.

7.11 Handling Unsupportive People

Not everyone will be happy about your decision to quit or reduce alcohol. Some might feel that you are judging them. Others might be used to you being the "party friend" and want things to stay the same. It can be painful when people you love are not behind your goals.

- **Stand Firm**: Be polite but firm in restating your choice. "I understand you want me to have a drink with you, but I'm taking care of my health now."
- **Avoid Arguing**: You do not have to debate or prove your point. If they keep pushing, it may be best to exit the conversation.
- **Limit Exposure**: If a certain person always tries to sabotage your plan, it might be necessary to reduce contact or avoid them in social settings for a while.

- **Seek Support Elsewhere**: If you cannot rely on that individual, turn to others who respect what you are doing.

7.12 Balancing Giving and Receiving

When you find a good support group or a supportive friend, it can be tempting to lean on them constantly. However, support works best when it is balanced. You receive help, but you also contribute in some way.

- **Offer Assistance**: If someone in your group is feeling low, send them an encouraging message. This not only helps them but can strengthen your own resolve.
- **Share Your Stories**: Hearing your ups and downs may help others feel less alone. You do not have to present yourself as perfect or always successful. Honesty can be more comforting than pretending everything is easy.
- **Respect Boundaries**: Your supporters have their own lives. They might not be free every time you want to talk. Have multiple sources of help so you do not overwhelm one person.
- **Be Thankful**: If someone goes out of their way to help you, show thanks. A genuine "thank you" or a small gesture of gratitude can keep the relationship healthy.

7.13 Online Communities and Forums

With the rise of the internet, you can connect with supporters across the globe. Online communities can be a strong complement to face-to-face support. They offer anonymity, which can be useful if you are not ready to share your situation with people close to you.

- **Pick Reputable Platforms**: Look for sites with moderators who keep discussions respectful. This ensures a safer space.
- **Read and Learn**: Before posting, you can read through existing threads or stories to learn how people handle challenges similar to yours.
- **Join Discussions**: You can ask questions, respond to others, or simply offer encouragement. Engaging in group conversations can create a sense of belonging.

- **Beware of Negative Spaces**: Some online places can be critical or full of arguments. If you find a forum that makes you feel worse, find a different one.

7.14 Mentor or Sponsor Relationships

In some support circles, you can connect with a mentor or sponsor. This is usually someone who has been sober or has handled their drinking problem for a while and can guide newcomers.

- **Experience and Tips**: A sponsor has likely faced common pitfalls and can warn you about them in advance.
- **One-on-One Contact**: You can call or text them during rough moments. Knowing someone is available can ease anxiety.
- **Shared Goals**: Sponsors remember what it was like to be in your shoes. They might help you set goals that are realistic and coach you on how to manage stress.
- **Respect Their Time**: Sponsors are volunteers. They often help multiple people. Follow any guidelines they provide about contact hours or emergency calls.

7.15 Creating Sober Social Circles

If your main group of friends centers on drinking, you might need to form new connections. A sober social circle means you can hang out without constantly dealing with peer pressure.

- **Local Clubs or Meetups**: Many cities have clubs for hobbies like hiking, board games, cooking, or fitness. These groups usually do not revolve around alcohol.
- **Volunteering**: Joining a volunteer project can help you meet like-minded people who value helping others.
- **Community Events**: Look out for fairs, art shows, or cultural events that do not emphasize drinking. This can open you to new activities and possible friendships.
- **Online to Offline**: If you meet supportive friends in an online forum who live nearby, you could plan safe outings together.

7.16 Support for Mental Health

Quitting alcohol can bring many emotional shifts. Some people might uncover deeper sadness or anxiety they were trying to hide with drinks. It is vital to have mental health support if needed.

- **Counseling Sessions**: A counselor can guide you through emotional barriers and help you find healthier ways to handle stress.
- **Group Therapy**: Different from general support groups, a group therapy session is led by a trained professional who helps manage discussion and gives structured exercises.
- **Medication**: In some cases, a doctor might suggest short-term medication to help stabilize moods or reduce strong anxiety. This is a personal decision to discuss carefully with a medical professional.
- **Mindful Practices**: Some find relief in simple relaxation methods or focusing exercises that reduce stress. This can be done in group settings or one-on-one with a mental health expert.

7.17 Navigating Social Media

Many people share details of their lives on platforms like Facebook, Instagram, or others. Social media can be a double-edged sword. On one hand, you can find communities that support your goal. On the other, you might see posts of parties and drinks that trigger old cravings.

- **Curate Your Feed**: Unfollow or mute accounts that glamorize heavy drinking. You can also follow pages that focus on sober living, healthy recipes, or fitness.
- **Set Boundaries on Usage**: Scrolling late at night can stir up feelings of missing out or sadness. Consider limiting screen time if it affects your mood.
- **Join Positive Groups**: There are private Facebook groups or other social media communities dedicated to sobriety or harm reduction. You can join these for tips and encouragement.
- **Avoid Arguments**: If someone ridicules your choice online, do not engage in back-and-forth fights. It can sap your energy and create more stress.

7.18 Partner or Spouse Involvement

If you have a romantic partner or spouse, they can be one of your strongest allies, or one of the biggest challenges, depending on their own habits and beliefs.

- **Joint Goals**: If your partner also wants to drink less or adopt healthier habits, you can support each other. Plan date nights that do not involve alcohol, like a picnic or an evening walk.
- **Open Dialog**: Let your partner know about your triggers. For instance, if you feel the urge to drink when you argue, work on communication tools that keep stress levels lower.
- **Respect Their Choices**: If your partner drinks in moderation and does not want to stop, set boundaries. Ask them to keep alcohol out of sight or not drink around you if it leads to strong cravings.
- **Couples Counseling**: If drinking has caused conflict in the relationship, a couple's counselor can help address trust issues, resentment, or misunderstandings.

7.19 Checking Your Progress with Support

A support system is not set in stone. Over time, some people might drift away or new members may join. It is good to step back occasionally and see if your support network is still helping you reach your goals.

- **Regular Self-Evaluation**: Ask yourself every month or two, "Do I feel supported by those around me?" "Do I have the help I need?"
- **Refreshing Connections**: If you have not talked to your mentor or accountability buddy in a while, reach out and schedule a catch-up call.
- **Adding New People**: You might find that as your life changes, you meet others who share similar habits. They can become part of your sober circle.
- **Letting Go of Negative Influences**: If someone continues to undermine your goals or create drama, it might be time to limit or end that relationship.

CHAPTER 8: MANAGING STRESS AND EMOTIONAL TRIGGERS

Quitting or reducing alcohol use often brings about a flood of emotions. You might feel relief or pride in your progress, but you may also face stress, tension, or moments of sadness. For many people, stress and emotional turmoil are key factors that lead to drinking. They try to relax, numb pain, or dodge problems by grabbing a bottle. In this chapter, we will discuss how to handle stress, difficult feelings, and common triggers without returning to old habits.

8.1 Why Stress Is Linked to Drinking

Stress is a normal part of life. We deal with challenges at work, conflicts in relationships, health issues, or financial problems. When stress builds up, some people turn to alcohol as a quick solution. It can bring a brief sense of relaxation or help distract from worries. However, this relief is temporary, and the original stress remains. Over time, the body and mind grow dependent on alcohol to cope.

Key Points:

- Drinking as a shortcut: Alcohol might help you feel calmer in the short run, but it does not solve the underlying issue.
- Stress triggers cravings: When your stress level spikes, your mind might look for past coping methods, leading you to think about drinking.
- Cycle of more stress: Drinking can create new problems (like health or relationship troubles), leading to even higher stress.

8.2 Identifying Your Emotional Triggers

Emotional triggers are situations, thoughts, or feelings that spark the urge to drink. You might notice a pattern: whenever you feel lonely, bored, or undervalued, you reach for a drink.

- **Common Emotional Triggers**:
    - Anger or frustration

- Sadness or grief
- Anxiety or panic
- Feeling bored or restless
- Shame or guilt
- **Tracking Your Moods**: Keep a small journal or use an app to note your moods throughout the day. Look for patterns that match with cravings or times you used to drink.
- **Being Aware of Negative Thoughts**: Sometimes, unhelpful thoughts can pop up (e.g., "I deserve a drink for dealing with this"), fueling the urge.

When you know your triggers, you can plan ahead. You can set up healthier ways to cope with them instead of turning to alcohol.

8.3 Healthy Outlets for Stress

If alcohol was your main stress reliever, you now need new outlets. These do not have to be complicated. Simple methods can be very effective.

1. **Physical Exercise**: Moving your body can reduce tension and boost mood. It could be a brisk walk, dancing, or yoga. Exercise releases endorphins which help you feel better.
2. **Creative Activities**: Art, writing, or playing music can serve as an emotional release. You do not need to be an expert; the point is to express yourself.
3. **Hobbies**: Joining a sports league, gardening, cooking, or learning a skill can direct your energy toward something productive.
4. **Social Connection**: Chatting with a friend, joining a club, or attending a local event can relieve stress by giving you a sense of belonging.

8.4 Breathing and Relaxation Methods

Deep breathing is a fast way to calm your body's stress response. When you breathe deeply, you send a signal to your brain that it can relax.

- **Deep Belly Breathing**: Sit comfortably, place a hand on your abdomen, and inhale slowly through your nose. Feel your belly expand. Then exhale slowly through your mouth. Repeat for a couple of minutes.

- **Guided Imagery**: Picture a calm place or memory in your mind. Slowly take in the details—what colors you see, what sounds you hear, how the air feels.
- **Muscle Relaxation**: Tighten and then release muscle groups in your body, starting from your toes and moving upward. This can help you notice where tension hides.
- **Short Breaks**: Even stepping away from a stressful activity for a few minutes to take 5-10 slow, controlled breaths can reset your mind.

8.5 Changing Unhelpful Thought Patterns

The mind can fall into traps, especially under stress. You might think in extremes: "I messed up one day of sobriety, so I'll never succeed." These thoughts can push you to drink again. Learning to recognize and adjust negative thinking is a valuable skill.

- **Common Traps**:
    - **Black-and-White Thinking**: Believing you are either perfect or a total failure.
    - **Overgeneralizing**: Using words like "always" or "never" in a rigid way: "I always mess up."
    - **Catastrophizing**: Imagining the worst-case outcome in every situation.
- **Reality Check**: Ask yourself, "Is this thought entirely true?" "Could there be another way to look at this?"
- **Alternative Statements**: Replace thoughts like, "I'm a failure," with, "I made a mistake, but I can learn and keep going."

Working with a therapist can help you master these techniques more quickly. But you can start on your own by writing down your negative thoughts and examining their accuracy.

8.6 Time Management to Reduce Stress

Being overwhelmed with tasks can ramp up stress. If you cannot manage your time well, you might end up feeling you have no control, which can trigger old habits.

- **Plan Your Day**: Use a simple planner or phone calendar. Schedule tasks with realistic time blocks. This helps reduce the chaos of last-minute rushing.
- **Prioritize**: Focus on the tasks that matter most first. Let go of tasks that are not urgent or important.
- **Take Breaks**: Working non-stop can cause burnout. Regular short breaks can refresh your mind and lower stress levels.
- **Say "No" When Needed**: Do not take on more commitments than you can handle. It is okay to politely turn down new responsibilities if you are already stretched thin.

8.7 Handling Anger in Healthy Ways

Anger is a strong emotion that can push people to drink in order to relax or forget the situation. But bottled-up anger can build over time.

- **Recognize Early Signs**: Are your shoulders tensing up? Is your heart rate climbing? Do you start to clench your fists? Being aware of these signs can help you step away before anger explodes.
- **Count to Ten**: It might sound cliché, but taking a moment to pause and breathe can keep anger from boiling over.
- **Channel It**: Physical outlets like hitting a punching bag, going for a run, or even scribbling on paper can release built-up tension.
- **Express Assertively, Not Aggressively**: If someone upsets you, calm down first. Then talk it out without insults or threats. Clearly say how you feel and what you need.

8.8 Coping with Sadness or Guilt

Sadness is another emotion that can lead to drinking, especially if you used alcohol to soothe feelings of loss or guilt in the past.

- **Allow Yourself to Feel**: Emotions are not dangerous. Trying to block them can prolong your pain. Give yourself permission to be sad when you need to be.
- **Talk It Out**: Speak with a friend or counselor about what is bothering you. Verbalizing can bring some relief.

- **Grief or Loss**: If you are mourning a loss, understand that it might take time to heal. Alcohol does not speed this process; it only pauses it temporarily.
- **Positive Reminders**: Make a short list of things you appreciate in your life. This small step can counter the hopeless feeling that sometimes comes with sadness.

8.9 Overcoming Boredom and Restlessness

Many people drink out of sheer boredom. They come home after work, have no plans, and turn to alcohol out of habit. To avoid this, you can:

1. **Plan Evening Activities**: Even if it is something minor like preparing a new recipe, reading a book, or practicing a hobby for 30 minutes.
2. **Stay Engaged**: Keep your mind or hands busy. Simple crafts, puzzles, or games can fill the gap.
3. **Social Connections**: Invite a friend for a coffee or a walk. Boredom often lessens when you spend time talking or doing things together.
4. **Online Learning**: Take free online courses or watch how-to videos on a topic you find interesting. This can give your evenings structure.

8.10 Building Resilience

Resilience means bouncing back from hardship without losing yourself. It is not about never feeling stress or sadness. It is about learning to handle these moments effectively.

- **Learning from Setbacks**: If you have a slip and drink, view it as data, not a total defeat. Ask, "What led me to slip? How can I avoid that situation or handle it better next time?"
- **Positive Self-Talk**: Cheering yourself on is not silly. Thoughts like, "I can handle this," or, "I have gotten through worse," can help you stay steady.
- **Focus on Action**: Instead of feeling hopeless, think, "What step can I take right now to improve this situation?" Even small actions can build momentum.
- **Seek Role Models**: Read or listen to stories of others who overcame challenges. Their experiences can inspire new ideas for your own struggles.

8.11 Dealing with Anxiety or Panic

Anxiety can pop up in social settings, at work, or even out of the blue. Alcohol might have been your go-to to calm your nerves. Now you need different methods.

- **Breathing Exercises**: Slowly inhale for four seconds, hold for a moment, then exhale for four seconds. Repeat.
- **Grounding Techniques**: Focus on the present. Name five things you see, four things you can touch, three things you can hear, and so on. This can pull your mind away from racing thoughts.
- **Limit Stimulants**: Caffeine can boost anxiety levels. Try cutting down on coffee, energy drinks, or high-sugar snacks.
- **Professional Help**: If anxiety persists, consider talking to a therapist. They can teach strategies like systematic desensitization or other proven methods.

8.12 Planning Ahead for Stressful Events

Certain events are known to be stressful. Holidays, family gatherings, or job reviews can trigger tension. Instead of waiting to feel overwhelmed, prepare.

- **Predict Triggers**: If you know a family member always brings up old arguments, plan how you will respond calmly or exit the conversation.
- **Safe Spaces**: If you are at a gathering, identify a quiet spot you can retreat to if things get tense. Take short breaks there to recharge.
- **Bring a Friend**: A supportive friend can help you handle the environment and give you an excuse to leave if you need a break.
- **Focus on Non-Alcoholic Choices**: Bring your own drinks if you are worried about the selection. That way, you have a comfortable option.

8.13 Rewards That Do Not Involve Alcohol

Many people used to treat themselves with a drink after a long day. Now that you are changing that pattern, you can replace it with different rewards.

- **Pampering**: A warm bath, a home spa session, or a calming face mask can feel refreshing.
- **Short Trips**: Plan a day trip or a small outing to a nearby park or museum.
- **Creative Indulgences**: Purchase art supplies, a coloring book, or a new novel.
- **Food Treat**: If you enjoy cooking, try a new healthy recipe. If you like sweets, savor a small serving of something nice (but try not to replace one habit with another extreme).

Make sure these rewards do not become another unhealthy habit. Moderation is key.

8.14 Relaxation Through Nature

Nature can be a calming force. Spending time outdoors, even briefly, can lower stress.

- **Daily Walks**: If possible, walk in a park or near greenery. Notice the colors, the sounds of birds, or the rustle of leaves.
- **Gardening**: Tending to plants can be soothing. It can also give you a sense of responsibility and focus.
- **Outdoor Hobbies**: Consider simple activities like fishing, bicycling, or nature photography. These can help you relax and possibly meet others who share your interests.
- **Fresh Air Breaks**: If you live in a busy city, try to find small pockets of nature or set aside time to visit local trails on weekends.

8.15 Mindful Listening and Observing

Mindfulness is paying attention to the present moment without judgment. It can ease stress and reduce the urge to escape through drinking.

- **Mindful Listening**: When talking to someone, try to fully focus on their words. Notice the tone of their voice, the expressions on their face. This reduces wandering thoughts.

- **Mindful Eating**: Instead of scarfing down meals, chew slowly and notice the flavors and textures. This can help with impulse control in other areas of life too.
- **Body Scan**: Close your eyes and mentally move from your head to your toes, noticing how each area feels. If you detect tension, breathe and allow it to soften.
- **Avoid Multitasking**: Doing many things at once can raise stress. Try handling tasks one by one, giving each full attention.

8.16 Finding Emotional Balance

Emotional balance does not mean never having strong feelings. It means learning to manage them so they do not push you toward old habits.

- **Validate Yourself**: If you are feeling anxious, do not scold yourself. Accept it: "I feel anxious right now. That is understandable given the situation."
- **Seek Perspective**: Sometimes writing a quick note helps: "This problem is tough, but I have handled tough problems before."
- **Avoid Bottling Emotions**: If you keep everything inside, the tension can grow. Talk to someone you trust or write in a journal to release some of the pressure.
- **Remember Temporary Nature**: Emotions change. Today's anxiety can ease by tomorrow. Recognizing that feelings are not permanent can reduce panic.

8.17 Learning to Say "No"

People might ask you to join in activities that do not align with your new lifestyle. You might feel stress trying to please them, which can spark a craving to cope. Learning to say "no" politely but firmly is a big part of self-care.

- **Practice Short Phrases**: "No thanks, I have other plans." "I'm focusing on my health right now."
- **Do Not Over-Explain**: You do not owe anyone a detailed excuse. A brief refusal is enough.
- **Confidence**: Sound sure of yourself. If you come across uncertain, some might keep pushing.

- **Repeat if Needed**: If the person persists, repeat your statement. Change the subject if necessary.

8.18 Using Support Systems for Emotional Struggles

Remember the supportive network we discussed in Chapter 7? Use it whenever stress builds.

- **Alert Your Accountability Buddy**: If you feel a craving coming on due to stress, send a quick text or call.
- **Check In with a Mentor**: Sponsors or mentors often have tips for handling specific emotional triggers.
- **Group Support**: If you attend regular meetings, bring up the problem in the group discussion. Hearing different viewpoints can spark solutions you never considered.
- **Professional Sessions**: If you notice certain emotions repeatedly lead to trouble, a counselor can provide targeted strategies.

8.19 Preventing Burnout

If you push yourself too hard in the early days of quitting or reducing alcohol, you can burn out mentally and emotionally. This can weaken your resolve when a big stressor appears.

- **Realistic Goals**: Do not expect perfection. Aim for progress.
- **Rest**: Sleep is vital. Lack of rest can amplify stress.
- **Fun and Leisure**: Schedule time for fun. This can prevent you from feeling like your entire life is just about avoiding alcohol.
- **Self-Compassion**: Treat yourself with kindness, as you would a friend in the same situation.

CHAPTER 9: PRACTICAL TIPS TO PREVENT SLIPS

In earlier chapters, we covered goal setting, handling withdrawal, building a support network, and managing stress. These are the core parts of quitting or reducing alcohol use. However, maintaining your progress can be an ongoing task. Even people who have stayed away from alcohol for weeks or months can slip if they face a sudden trigger or if they become too relaxed about their habits. This chapter will focus on practical tips to avoid a slip, spot warning signs, and quickly recover if a slip does happen. We will go through methods you can use in daily life, as well as strategies for special events or unplanned triggers.

9.1 Why Slips Happen

Slips usually happen when a situation catches you off guard, when emotional states overwhelm your coping skills, or when old habits creep back in. Some common reasons include:

1. **Unmanaged Stress**: If you have ongoing worries about work, money, or relationships, you might start thinking that one drink could help calm your nerves.
2. **Overconfidence**: After a period of success, it is easy to think you have everything under control. You might test yourself by going to drinking spots or keeping alcohol in the house.
3. **Sudden Emotional Shocks**: Unexpected news or conflicts can knock you off balance. Without a plan, it is natural to return to old patterns.
4. **Social Pressure**: Friends or family might still offer you drinks, not fully respecting your new rules.
5. **Boredom or Loneliness**: Quiet evenings can lead to restlessness, making you recall how you used to fill that time with alcohol.

Remember that slipping does not mean failing. It is a sign that you need to review your strategies and strengthen certain areas.

9.2 Knowing Your Early Warning Signs

A slip rarely comes out of nowhere. Often, there are clues:

- **Thinking About Alcohol Often**: You may find your mind wandering to memories of drinking. You begin to romanticize it, forgetting the harm it caused.
- **Neglecting Support**: You skip meetings, ignore messages from your accountability buddies, or stop talking to supportive friends.
- **Feeling Above the Rules**: You might decide you can handle visiting your old drinking spots or hanging out with friends who drink heavily, without caution.
- **Irritability or Mood Swings**: Changes in mood could signal that you are not coping well with stress. If you are frequently upset or sad, it can lower your defenses.
- **Making Excuses**: Phrases like "Just one drink won't hurt," or "I deserve this because I'm stressed," are big red flags.

When you spot these signs, it is crucial to take action right away. Talk to someone you trust, review your goals, and consider adjusting your routine to handle the newfound risk.

9.3 Strengthening Daily Habits

Daily habits act like a shield. They help you live in a structured way that leaves less room for impulsive behavior.

1. **Morning Check-Ins**: Each morning, spend a minute or two asking yourself how you feel, what challenges might come up, and how you plan to avoid a slip.
2. **Regular Meals**: Low blood sugar or hunger can worsen cravings. Eat balanced meals at scheduled times to stay physically steady.
3. **Exercise or Activity**: Even light activities like walking or stretching can reduce tension and improve mood.
4. **Healthy Distractions**: Keep quick, stress-free tasks nearby (puzzles, simple chores, short reading sessions). When you sense an urge, divert your attention to these tasks.

5. **Wind-Down Routine**: Close the day with relaxing music, a warm bath, or quiet reading. Keep away from screens right before bed if they heighten anxiety.

These daily routines serve as anchors that keep you steady, especially during high-stress periods.

9.4 Action Plans for Risky Settings

Sometimes you cannot avoid a place where alcohol is present. It might be a work party, a family gathering, or a wedding. In these cases, plan in advance.

- **Set a Time Limit**: Decide how long you will stay. If it is a two-hour dinner, you might choose to leave after the meal rather than hang around for the drinks.
- **Take a Safe Buddy**: If possible, bring along someone who respects your decision. They can support you if you feel uneasy or want to leave early.
- **Control Your Own Drink**: Keep a non-alcoholic drink in your hand. This helps you turn down offers because you can say you already have a beverage.
- **Map Out an Exit**: Know where your car, bus stop, or ride service pickup is. If you feel uneasy, exit quickly instead of trying to "tough it out."
- **Avoid Drinking Games**: If everyone is playing a game centered on alcohol, either step away or suggest a different activity that does not involve drinking.

By having a plan, you are less likely to be taken by surprise and more likely to handle the event on your own terms.

9.5 Avoiding Triggers in Media and Advertising

Alcohol ads or scenes in movies can sometimes trigger cravings. It might look glamorous or give you memories of the "good times" with drinking. Here are ways to limit that effect:

1. **Use Technology Filters**: Some apps or browser extensions can block certain ads or content.

2. **Choose TV Shows Wisely**: If a show repeatedly focuses on partying or heavy drinking, switch to something less triggering.
3. **Stay Alert**: When you see an alcohol commercial, remind yourself of why you stopped. It might help to repeat a phrase like, "I remember what this really did to me."
4. **Avoid Certain Social Media**: If you follow accounts that always highlight drinking, consider unfollowing or muting them.

These steps might seem small, but they prevent constant exposure to triggers that can undermine your resolve.

9.6 Safe Alternatives to Alcohol

If you are used to having a drink in the evening or during social events, it can help to find tasty and interesting non-alcoholic drinks. This is not about hiding from alcohol, but about giving yourself a better option.

- **Mocktails**: You can mix fruit juices, sparkling water, or soda with fresh herbs and garnishes to create fun drinks.
- **Flavored Teas**: There are many varieties of herbal or fruit-infused teas that can taste satisfying.
- **Homemade Smoothies**: Blend fresh fruit, yogurt, and ice for a refreshing treat.
- **Infused Water**: Add slices of lemon, cucumber, or berries to a pitcher of water and let it sit in the fridge.
- **Sparkling Water with Extras**: Squeeze in lime, lemon, or orange juice for a quick, bubbly refreshment.

These substitutes can lessen the sense of missing out when others drink, especially at gatherings.

9.7 Small Rewards for Consistent Effort

When you reach a goal like a full week or month without a slip, give yourself a simple, healthy reward. This approach keeps you motivated. Instead of "just one drink" as a reward, pick something that does not break your progress.

- **Practical Treats**: Perhaps buy a new book, try a new recipe, or get a small piece of fitness equipment.
- **Outdoor Activity**: Plan a short outing to a local park, beach, or hiking trail (if you enjoy outdoor activities).
- **Creative Fun**: Maybe sign up for a basic art workshop or an online class related to something you have always wanted to learn.

These pleasant activities can give you a sense of achievement. They also remind you that life without alcohol can still be enjoyable and fulfilling.

9.8 Being Honest About Slips

If a slip does occur, honesty is key. Hiding it or pretending it did not happen can trap you in shame and secrecy, which increases the risk of more slips.

1. **Tell a Supporter**: Share with a trusted friend, counselor, or support group member. Let them know what happened and how you feel.
2. **Review Circumstances**: Reflect on the exact situation, mood, and thought patterns leading up to the slip. This is not about blaming yourself; it is about learning.
3. **Adjust Your Plan**: Once you see what went wrong, tweak your routines or strategies to reduce the risk next time. Maybe you need to skip certain social events or text a friend before going.
4. **Watch Out for Shame**: A slip does not wipe out all your progress. Consider how far you have come. Guilt can drag you down, but looking at it as a chance to improve your plan can lift you back up.

9.9 Keeping a "Slips and Solutions" Journal

A practical tool can be a small notebook or digital file where you write down any slip or near-slip events. You can note the date, location, who was with you, how you felt, and what thoughts were in your mind. Then, in another column, you can brainstorm solutions.

- **Example Entry**:
  - Slip: Drank a glass of wine at a friend's birthday.
  - Reason: Felt pressured and did not want to look rude.

- Solution: Next time, bring my own non-alcoholic drink and openly mention my new plan at the start so no one offers me alcohol.

This method helps you see patterns and keeps solutions fresh in your mind.

9.10 Engaging the Senses

When a craving strikes, try using your senses to stay in the moment and reduce the intensity of the urge.

- **Taste**: Chew gum or a strong mint. The sudden flavor can shift your focus away from alcohol.
- **Smell**: Use a calming scent like lavender or chamomile. Some people keep a small vial of scented oil on hand.
- **Touch**: Hold a stress ball or a worry stone in your hand. The tactile feedback can ground you.
- **Hearing**: Listen to a favorite song, a motivational podcast, or even a relaxing nature sound track.
- **Sight**: Look at something you find peaceful—photos of loved ones, nature pictures, or artwork. Slow down and really observe the details.

This approach can "interrupt" the craving, giving you time to recall your goals and make a healthier choice.

9.11 Rehearsing Situations

Many performers or athletes practice for events in their minds before they happen. You can apply a similar technique to prepare for high-risk situations.

- **Visualize**: Imagine going to a party or a stressful family gathering. Picture yourself refusing drinks confidently, then leaving feeling proud.
- **Imagine Hurdles**: Also think about possible pitfalls. What if someone hands you a drink insistently? How will you respond? Rehearse your polite refusal.
- **Positive End Scene**: End the mental practice with a successful outcome—walking away sober, feeling in control, and returning home safe.

This mental run-through can give you a sense of readiness, so you are not caught off guard.

9.12 Setting Boundaries with Others

Sometimes, the people around you might not respect your decision to stay away from alcohol. You might need to set limits to protect yourself.

- **Explain Calmly**: Let them know you are serious about your choice. If they tease you, respond plainly that you do not find it amusing and that you need their support, not their jokes.
- **Limit Contact**: If certain relatives or friends refuse to respect your boundaries, consider spending less time with them until you are more stable in your new habits.
- **Handle Arguments**: If they become confrontational, you can politely end the conversation or remove yourself from the location. You do not have to prove yourself to them.

This might feel tough or awkward, but standing up for your needs is important for preventing slips.

9.13 Using Technology for Accountability

In the digital age, there are many apps and online platforms that can help you maintain your progress.

- **Sobriety Tracker Apps**: These apps let you log the days you stay away from alcohol. Some show you money saved or days gained.
- **Reminder Apps**: Set alarms or notifications for times of the day you tend to feel cravings. Have a brief motivational note pop up, like: "You are stronger than this urge."
- **Online Communities**: If you cannot attend a face-to-face support group, consider joining an online group where you can post updates or ask for help in real time.
- **Virtual Meetups**: Video calls with supportive friends or mentors can be as encouraging as in-person meetings when used regularly.

Technology can be a useful companion, keeping you focused and making it easier to reach out for help at any hour.

9.14 Regular Health Checkups

Physical health problems can create stress, making a slip more likely. As you cut down on alcohol, remember to schedule routine checkups with your doctor or any relevant specialists.

1. **Blood Tests**: Checking liver function and other markers can help you see how your body is improving or if something needs extra care.
2. **Discuss Vitamins**: Some people might be low on certain nutrients due to past drinking. A doctor can recommend supplements if needed.
3. **Medication Interactions**: If you take any medications, let your doctor know about your alcohol history to avoid negative interactions.
4. **Honesty with Healthcare Providers**: Be open about your progress and any slips. They can give you guidance without judging.

Keeping track of your health can offer extra motivation as well. Seeing improvements in your blood work or energy levels reminds you why this change is worth the effort.

9.15 Scheduled Check-Ins with Yourself

Make it a habit to do a bigger review of your progress weekly or monthly. Ask yourself:

- **What went well?** Perhaps you passed on drinks at a party or felt more relaxed handling stress at work.
- **Where did I struggle?** Did you feel intense cravings after an argument, or did a friend's teasing get to you?
- **Do I need new strategies?** Maybe you found a new trigger or realized a new coping method could help.
- **Am I using my support network effectively?** Sometimes, you might forget you have people or resources ready to assist.

These check-ins keep you mindful and prevent you from drifting away from your plan.

9.16 Avoiding Complacency Over Time

Over months or years, if you have been steady without major slips, you might start believing you are fully immune to the lure of alcohol. This sense of complacency can be dangerous.

1. **Continue Routines**: Even if you feel strong, do not drop your daily and weekly habits. They are the foundation that got you here.
2. **Stay Informed**: Read articles, watch short talks, or keep up with recovery-related information. This ensures you remain aware of ongoing strategies and developments.
3. **Periodic Support Meetings**: Even if you no longer feel you need them every week, dropping by a support meeting once a month can help you stay grounded.
4. **Give Back**: Helping others who are starting out can remind you of how far you have come and why you do not want to slip back.

Remaining careful does not mean living in fear. It simply means respecting how powerful alcohol can be and staying on guard in a healthy, balanced way.

9.17 Quick Tools for Urgent Moments

Sometimes, you will have a strong urge out of nowhere. It might hit you when you are alone or upset. Here are a few quick techniques you can try on the spot:

- **Count Down and Distract**: Count backward from 20 slowly. When you reach 1, shift your focus to a different activity, like a quick chore, a breathing exercise, or a simple puzzle.
- **Phone a Friend**: If you have someone who is okay with a sudden call, dial their number and say, "I'm feeling the urge right now. Can we talk?"
- **Sip Water Slowly**: Drinking water in small sips can calm the body. Focus on the sensation of the water and how it feels.
- **Chew Something Strong**: Keep gum or crunchy snacks handy. The strong flavor or texture can pull your attention away from the craving.

These tips might sound small, but they can defuse urges that otherwise might build into a slip.

9.18 Reminding Yourself of the Consequences

When a craving pops up, the mind often recalls the short-term good feelings of alcohol. It might forget the harmful outcomes. Reminding yourself of the full picture is important.

- **List the Negatives**: Keep a short list (mental or written) of all the problems caused by drinking: health issues, lost money, regrets, relationship problems, or legal troubles.
- **Look at Old Photos**: Some people keep pictures of themselves from a time when alcohol caused them to look unwell or when they were in a negative place. Seeing that can jolt the mind back to reality.
- **Remember the Hangovers**: Think about the mornings you woke up feeling awful or the times you felt embarrassed about your behavior. These memories can help squash the urge to give in.

9.19 Building a Bigger Purpose

A helpful way to prevent slips is to focus on something larger than just "not drinking." If you have a bigger purpose or set of goals in your life, you might be less tempted to risk them.

1. **Work or Career**: Strive for improvement in your job or look for ways to build a new skill that could expand your opportunities.
2. **Service**: Helping others through volunteering or community efforts can give you a sense of meaning and responsibility.
3. **Family Goals**: Perhaps you want to be a healthier, more present parent or partner.
4. **Long-Term Projects**: This could be saving for a house, training for a fitness event, or writing a personal journal. Having a big project gives you motivation to stay on track.

Having meaningful aims keeps you forward-focused, which can reduce the appeal of old habits.

CHAPTER 10: BALANCED NUTRITION AND SELF-CARE

Your physical state can have a strong effect on your mental well-being and your determination to stay away from alcohol. When the body is undernourished or in poor health, you might feel fatigued, irritable, or anxious. These states can trigger cravings. Conversely, when your body has the nutrients and rest it needs, you can think more clearly, regulate emotions better, and handle stress without turning to alcohol. This chapter will guide you through balanced eating, hydration, exercise, and other elements of self-care. We will cover easy steps you can integrate into your routine, plus some pointers that might be less obvious but highly beneficial.

10.1 Why Nutrition Matters After Cutting Alcohol

When a person has been drinking heavily, their diet often lacks important vitamins and minerals. Alcohol is full of empty calories, meaning it can fill you up without giving your body the nutrients it needs. Over time, this can cause deficiencies that affect organs, mental function, and energy levels.

- **Replacing Lost Nutrients**: Vitamins like B1 (thiamine), B6, and folate can be lower than normal in people who drink regularly. Restoring these can help improve mood and mental clarity.
- **Stable Blood Sugar**: Alcohol can throw off your blood sugar balance. Eating balanced meals helps stabilize energy, reducing cravings triggered by feeling shaky or weak.
- **Reducing Cravings**: A well-fed body is less likely to seek quick fixes like alcohol. Nutritious foods keep hunger and cravings under better control.

Focusing on nourishing meals can speed up your body's recovery, letting you gain energy and vitality you might not have felt for a long time.

10.2 Building a Balanced Meal

A balanced meal typically includes protein, healthy carbohydrates, and good fats, plus vitamins and minerals from fruits or vegetables.

1. **Protein Sources**: Lean meats (chicken, turkey), fish, eggs, beans, or tofu. Protein helps rebuild tissues and maintains muscle.
2. **Complex Carbs**: Brown rice, whole wheat bread, oats, or quinoa. These break down slower, keeping your blood sugar stable.
3. **Healthy Fats**: Avocados, nuts, seeds, or certain oils (olive, canola). Fats help with hormone production and can make meals more satisfying.
4. **Vegetables and Fruits**: They add fiber, vitamins, and minerals. A variety of colors can help ensure you get a broad range of nutrients.
5. **Adequate Fluids**: Water, herbal teas, or low-sugar beverages. Avoid sugary drinks that might cause spikes in energy followed by crashes.

This kind of meal plan does not have to be boring or expensive. Even simple choices like grilled chicken, roasted veggies, and brown rice can support your body's healing.

10.3 Hydration and Its Role

Water is crucial for many functions in the body. When you quit alcohol, you might notice changes in fluid balance. Some people might have used alcohol as a main beverage, leading to dehydration. Now is the time to correct that.

- **Aim for Steady Intake**: A common guideline is about 6–8 cups (1.5–2 liters) of water per day, but individual needs vary.
- **Add Flavor**: If plain water feels dull, add slices of lemon, cucumber, or a few berries to keep it interesting.
- **Watch for Signs of Dehydration**: Dark-colored urine, headaches, or dry mouth can indicate you need more fluids.
- **Other Drinks**: Tea, coffee, and milk also contribute to hydration, though be mindful of caffeine if you are prone to anxiety.

Staying well-hydrated helps your body flush out toxins and maintain clear thinking, which supports your alcohol-free plan.

10.4 Specific Nutrients to Consider

As you improve your diet, you may want to pay extra attention to these nutrients, which are often low in people who used to drink heavily:

1. **Thiamine (Vitamin B1)**: Helps your body convert food into energy. Low levels can cause fatigue and nerve problems. Foods like whole grains, legumes, and some seeds contain B1.
2. **Folate**: Important for cell repair and growth. Leafy greens, beans, and citrus fruits have good amounts.
3. **Magnesium**: Plays a role in muscle function and mood regulation. Found in nuts, seeds, whole grains, and leafy greens.
4. **Zinc**: Affects immune function and wound healing. Sources include meat, shellfish, seeds, and whole grains.
5. **Vitamin D**: Helps with bone health and mood. You can get it from sunlight (in safe amounts) and certain foods like fatty fish or fortified products.

Before taking supplements, consider talking to a doctor or dietitian. They can test for deficiencies and guide you on appropriate doses.

10.5 Healthy Snacking

One potential challenge when quitting alcohol is resisting sugary or unhealthy snacks. The body might crave quick energy if it is used to getting extra calories from drinks. To avoid replacing one harmful habit with another, plan your snacks wisely.

- **Keep Fruits Handy**: Apples, berries, or bananas can satisfy a sweet craving.
- **Protein-Rich Snacks**: Yogurt, cottage cheese, a small handful of nuts, or hummus with vegetables can keep you satisfied longer.
- **Whole Grain Choices**: Crackers or a small piece of whole wheat bread with peanut butter can be a balanced mini-meal.
- **Limit Chips and Candy**: These can give a short burst of energy followed by a crash. If you do indulge, watch the portion size.

Having healthy snacks ready makes it easier to stay on track when hunger strikes between meals.

10.6 The Role of Regular Meal Times

Skipping meals can cause low energy or irritability, which can lead you to seek relief in a drink. Keeping a routine for meal times helps stabilize your mood and blood sugar.

1. **Breakfast**: Even something simple like oatmeal or whole wheat toast with a boiled egg can jump-start your day.
2. **Lunch**: Aim for balance—perhaps a sandwich with lean protein, plus vegetables or soup.
3. **Dinner**: Choose a satisfying mix of protein, carbs, and vegetables.
4. **Small Snacks**: If needed, space them between meals to avoid extreme hunger.

Knowing your next meal is coming can reduce stress about what to eat and helps you avoid impulsive, unhealthy choices.

10.7 Light to Moderate Exercise

Movement helps in many ways: it raises mood, lowers stress, supports weight balance, and can distract you from cravings. You do not have to become a fitness expert to gain these benefits.

- **Walking**: This is one of the simplest forms of exercise. You can start with a short walk around the block and slowly increase the distance.
- **Low-Impact Workouts**: Swimming or cycling can be easy on the joints while giving you a good workout.
- **Home Exercises**: Bodyweight exercises like squats, lunges, or push-ups can be done at home with minimal equipment.
- **Group Activities**: Joining a local sports league, dance class, or exercise group can keep you motivated and help you make new friends.
- **Stretching or Yoga**: Helps with flexibility, breathing, and mental calmness. There are many beginner-friendly videos online.

Always listen to your body. If you have any health concerns, check with a doctor before starting a new exercise program.

10.8 Sleep and Rest

Proper sleep might have been disturbed by alcohol. While it can make people feel drowsy at first, alcohol disrupts deep sleep. Now that you are drinking less or none, you may need to re-teach your body to sleep well.

- **Set a Bedtime**: Going to bed and waking up at the same time each day helps regulate your internal clock.
- **Limit Screens**: The light from phones and computers can interfere with the sleep hormone. Try to switch them off an hour before bed.
- **Avoid Heavy Meals Before Bed**: Large late-night meals can make it hard to fall asleep.
- **Create a Calming Routine**: A warm shower, dim lighting, or listening to soft music can signal your brain that it is time to wind down.

Getting quality sleep can help regulate mood, reduce stress, and make it easier to handle the day without cravings.

10.9 Mindful Eating Practices

Mindful eating means paying close attention to the taste, texture, and smell of your food. It can help prevent overeating or emotional snacking.

- **Slow Down**: Put your fork down between bites. This gives your brain time to register fullness.
- **Focus on Food**: Avoid watching TV or scrolling your phone while eating. Pay attention to each bite.
- **Savor Flavors**: Notice the sweetness of a piece of fruit or the spices in a dish. This can increase satisfaction, reducing the urge to keep munching mindlessly.
- **Check Your Emotions**: If you find yourself heading to the fridge when you are stressed or bored, pause and ask, "Am I really hungry or just seeking comfort?"

Mindful eating can help you enjoy meals more while staying in tune with your body's signals.

10.10 Relaxation and Stress-Reduction

Stress can easily derail both nutrition and sobriety goals. Adding simple relaxation tools to your routine can keep cortisol (the stress hormone) in check.

1. **Breathing Exercises**: We mentioned these before, but they are worth revisiting. A few deep breaths can reset tension quickly.
2. **Light Stretches**: If you work at a desk, stand up every hour or two for a quick stretch. Loosen your shoulders, neck, and back.
3. **Journaling**: Write down worries or tasks to get them off your mind. This can help you identify patterns in your daily stress.
4. **Short Breaks**: Even a 5-minute walk outside or a few moments to look at a peaceful photo can lower anxiety.

A calmer mind is less likely to crave alcohol or junk food for instant comfort.

10.11 Personal Grooming and Self-Care Rituals

Sometimes, when people drink regularly, they let their personal grooming or self-care routines slip. Reintroducing these can help you feel more confident and positive about life without alcohol.

- **Skin Care**: Cleansing and moisturizing your skin can be a simple daily routine that feels soothing.
- **Hair Care**: Regular trims or trying a simple new style can boost how you feel about your appearance.
- **Hands and Feet**: Basic nail care or an occasional soak can be relaxing.
- **Comfortable Clothing**: Wearing clean, comfortable clothes can remind you that you deserve to feel good, inside and out.

These small habits can help you sense your own worth, which in turn strengthens your resolve.

10.12 Filling Your Time with Positive Activities

One of the traps after quitting alcohol is having a lot more free time and not knowing what to do with it. If you do not fill that gap, boredom can lead to cravings. So consider:

- **Hobbies**: Try out a new craft, cooking style, or online classes for a subject that sparks your interest.
- **Volunteering**: Helping at a local charity or community center can give you structure and a sense of purpose.
- **Group Outings**: Join hiking clubs, book clubs, or sports teams that do not center on alcohol.
- **Creative Arts**: Painting, writing, or even adult coloring books can be calm and satisfying activities.

Engaging in positive pursuits keeps you moving forward, away from the lifestyle you left behind.

10.13 Mental Health Check-Ins

As you improve your health, keep an eye on your mental well-being. Some might see improvements quickly; others need more time. If you notice persistent sadness, anxiety, or hopelessness, it may be wise to get professional support.

- **Therapy**: A counselor can help you address emotional concerns and suggest coping techniques.
- **Support Groups**: Sharing with others who have faced similar challenges can reduce feelings of isolation.
- **Medication**: In some cases, a doctor might suggest short-term or long-term medication to manage conditions like anxiety or sadness.
- **Activities That Spark Joy**: Do not forget small pleasures, whether it is listening to music you love or taking a peaceful walk in nature.

Looking after your mental health is as vital as taking care of your physical body.

10.14 Limiting Caffeine and Sugar

Some people who quit alcohol notice they start leaning heavily on coffee, soda, or sugary snacks. While these are not as harmful as alcohol, consuming too much can still impact your energy and mood.

- **Caffeine**: Too much can make you jittery and disrupt your sleep. If you notice this, consider cutting back or limiting caffeine to earlier in the day.
- **Sugary Foods**: They can cause spikes and crashes in blood sugar, leading to mood swings. Try to stick to natural sugars (fruit) or moderate portions of sweet treats.
- **Gradual Changes**: You do not need to stop caffeine or sugar altogether suddenly. Slow reductions might be easier to handle without feeling deprived.

Keeping these in moderation helps you stay calm and balanced.

10.15 Kitchen Organization

A small but helpful tip is to organize your kitchen in a way that supports your new lifestyle:

1. **Stock Healthy Essentials**: Have fresh vegetables, fruits, lean proteins, and whole grains at your fingertips.
2. **Limit Junk Food**: If it is not in your house, you will not reach for it out of habit.
3. **Set Up a Hydration Station**: Keep a jug of cold water or herbal tea ready in the fridge. If it is easy to access, you are more likely to drink it.
4. **Meal Prepping**: Cook batches of food and store in single-portion containers. This helps avoid grabbing takeout or skipping meals when you are busy.

A well-arranged kitchen can reduce daily decision-making stress, leaving you more energy for other positive actions.

10.16 Rewarding Progress with Non-Food Items

While it is normal to occasionally treat yourself to a special dessert, do not rely only on food rewards. Look for non-food ways to mark your successes:

- **Experience Gifts**: Treat yourself to a museum pass, a local event, or a class you want to take.
- **Comfort Items**: Maybe a new pillow, a soft blanket, or a pair of cozy socks.
- **Small Décor**: A houseplant or a small piece of art can bring life to your home.
- **Relaxation Tools**: Scented candles, bath salts, or a simple foot massager can help create a spa-like vibe at home.

This keeps the focus on overall well-being rather than eating or drinking to celebrate.

10.17 Tracking Your Improvements

Keeping a simple log or journal of your wellness habits can help you see how far you have come. You can note:

1. **Daily Food Intake**: Not in a strict calorie-counting way, but just to see if you are getting a balanced variety.
2. **Water Consumption**: You might mark how many cups or bottles of water you finish.
3. **Exercise**: Log what type of activity you did and for how long.
4. **Sleep**: Record bedtime, wake time, and how rested you feel in the morning.

Seeing positive changes can encourage you to stay with your new routine. It also reveals patterns—like if you tend to eat worse on certain days or if missing sleep leads to more cravings.

10.18 Balancing Work, Family, and Personal Time

Self-care also means scheduling enough time for yourself. If you work nonstop or have many family responsibilities, you can burn out and become susceptible to cravings.

- **Set Clear Hours**: If possible, define when you are "on" (working) and when you are "off."
- **Delegate Tasks**: Let family members or coworkers handle tasks that do not need your direct input.
- **Short Personal Breaks**: Even ten minutes to read a book, listen to music, or just breathe can restore energy levels.
- **Mindful Home Routines**: Meal planning or cleaning can become more manageable when shared among household members.

Striking a balance keeps you from feeling overwhelmed and helps maintain mental clarity.

10.19 Possible Challenges and How to Handle Them

While focusing on good nutrition and self-care, you may run into obstacles:

- **Budget Limits**: Nutritious foods can be affordable if you plan wisely. Look for sales, buy frozen fruits and vegetables, and cook in batches.
- **Limited Time**: Quick-cooking methods, meal prepping on weekends, or using a slow cooker can save time.
- **Lack of Cooking Skills**: Simple tutorials online can teach you basic techniques. Start with easy recipes that use just a few ingredients.
- **Social Situations**: Friends might invite you to fancy restaurants or bars. Suggest alternative options or pick a healthy meal when you go out. If they drink, stick to your plan of non-alcoholic drinks.

Overcoming these hurdles can give you a sense of achievement that goes hand-in-hand with your progress in quitting alcohol.

CHAPTER 11: BUILDING NEW ROUTINES AND HOBBIES

Quitting alcohol often creates empty spaces in your daily life. You might have spent a lot of time thinking about drinking, actually drinking, or recovering from its effects. Once you remove alcohol from the picture, you can find yourself with extra hours or a gap in your usual schedule. This gap can feel strange. It might lead to boredom or restlessness if you do not fill it with something else. That is where new routines and hobbies come in. By directing your time and attention to better activities, you can add structure to your day and find healthy outlets for stress or free time.

Building a new routine does not have to be difficult. It simply means creating steady habits that help you live in a way that supports your decision to quit or reduce alcohol. Hobbies can be the fun side of this. They give you something interesting to learn or do. It can be a hobby you used to enjoy but stopped, or a completely new skill you want to explore. This chapter will lay out ways to find, set up, and maintain routines and hobbies that lift your mood, expand your social circle if desired, and keep you focused on healthy living.

11.1 Why Building New Routines Matters

A routine is a pattern of behavior that repeats daily or weekly. For example, you might wake up, stretch, have breakfast, head to work or school, and so on. When you had an alcohol habit, drinking might have been a fixed part of that pattern: "When I come home from work, I drink." Removing that piece can feel unsettling, like you are missing part of your day. Replacing the old behavior with a healthier one helps you stay clear of triggers.

Routines also bring predictability. Many people find comfort in having set times for meals, exercise, relaxation, and social connections. This predictability can lower stress. It can also give you little goals to meet each day, which helps you feel accomplished. For instance, if your routine is to walk in the park for 20 minutes after dinner, you have a simple action that keeps you active. That one habit can anchor the rest of your evening.

11.2 Understanding the Role of Hobbies

Hobbies are enjoyable activities that you do in your free time. They can be creative or physical, social or quiet. The key is that they bring positive feelings and keep you engaged. Hobbies can serve several purposes in your alcohol-free life:

1. **Stress Outlet**: Many hobbies, like painting, writing, or playing a musical instrument, allow you to release tension or express emotions.
2. **Social Connection**: Team sports or group classes can help you meet people who share an interest, expanding your support circle.
3. **Sense of Achievement**: Learning a new skill can be fulfilling, boosting your self-esteem and reminding you that you can grow in many ways.
4. **Structured Free Time**: Even if you pick a simple hobby like puzzle-solving, it can fill empty hours that once led you to think about drinking.

Finding a hobby that fits your personality and interests is a step toward a well-rounded life without alcohol.

11.3 Shifting Old Patterns

In the past, you might have come home and instantly poured a drink. That pattern can be tough to break if you do not introduce something new. Here are ideas on how to shift the old pattern:

- **Replace the Trigger Time**: If your usual drinking time was right after work, plan a quick walk, gym visit, or simple home exercise session. By doing that right away, you fill the time when you would usually grab a drink.
- **Change Locations**: If you often drank in the kitchen, try rearranging the furniture or spending more time in another room. Changing your environment can help break the association.
- **Set Alerts**: If you struggle with forgetting your new plan, put an alarm on your phone to remind you: "Go for a 15-minute walk" or "Make a fruit smoothie." This can interrupt the old habit loop.

Over time, these small changes become normal to you. You will find that not drinking at that time feels natural once a new habit is in place.

11.4 Step-by-Step Approach to Creating a New Routine

1. **Identify a Target Activity**: Decide what you want to do instead of drinking. It could be a light activity like stretching, reading a chapter of a book, or working on a short creative project.
2. **Pick a Regular Time**: This new activity should happen at roughly the same time each day to become a habit. Maybe it is 6 p.m. on weekdays or right after dinner.
3. **Keep It Simple**: Do not overcomplicate it. If your replacement behavior is too hard or time-consuming, you might give up quickly. Start with something you can manage easily.
4. **Track Your Progress**: Use a small calendar, an app, or a notebook to note each day you follow through. Seeing that streak grow can be encouraging.
5. **Review and Adjust**: If you find the activity does not excite you after a week or two, switch it up. The goal is to find a routine you can stick with.

Remember, routines need to be practical.

11.5 Brainstorming New Hobbies

Choosing a new hobby does not have to be complicated. It helps to think about your personal likes or curiosities:

1. **Look at Your Past Interests**: Were there things you enjoyed as a child or teenager? Maybe you used to draw, build models, or play a sport. These could be great to revisit.
2. **Survey Your Current Life**: Is there a topic you find yourself reading about or watching videos on? That might be a sign you would enjoy turning it into a hobby.
3. **Ask Friends or Family**: Sometimes, people around you can see talents or interests you do not notice in yourself.
4. **Browse Community Classes**: Check local listings or online sites for beginner classes. You might find cooking lessons, pottery sessions, or group dance classes.
5. **Try Small Samples**: If you are unsure, pick a short, basic project. For example, if you think you might enjoy knitting, buy a simple starter kit and see how it feels.

Brainstorming is about seeing what fits your lifestyle. You do not have to commit to a hobby forever. A few trials can point you toward the one that really grabs you.

11.6 Low-Cost or Free Hobbies

Some people worry that hobbies cost too much money. While certain hobbies can be pricey, many are cheap or even free:

- **Walking or Jogging**: You only need comfortable shoes. Local parks or sidewalks are free to use.
- **Reading**: Libraries lend books for free. You can also borrow e-books from many library systems.
- **Online Tutorials**: Many websites offer free lessons on languages, art, coding, and more.
- **Gardening**: A small container garden on a balcony can be cheap if you use seeds and simple supplies.
- **Volunteer Work**: Helping out at an animal shelter or community group is not only free but also gives a sense of purpose.
- **Board Games or Card Games**: If you already own a set of cards or a board game, you can enjoy hours of fun without extra cost.

Cost does not have to hold you back from finding a new interest that enriches your life.

11.7 Social Hobbies vs. Solo Hobbies

Some hobbies are social—team sports, group dance classes, or group walks—while others are more personal, like painting, reading, or writing. Both types have benefits:

- **Social Hobbies**: They can help you meet new people, which might replace old drinking buddies who still indulge in alcohol. You can form connections based on the shared activity rather than on drinking.
- **Solo Hobbies**: These can give you quiet time to unwind, reflect, or rest if you have a busy schedule. Solo activities like crafting or writing can help clear your mind.

You might try a mix of both. Some days you may want to join a club or sports group, and on others, you might enjoy reading a book alone. Balance is the key.

11.8 Overcoming Fear of Trying New Things

It is common to feel nervous when starting a new activity, especially if you think you might not be good at it. This fear can block you from exploring new pastimes that might bring joy or relaxation.

- **Keep Expectations Realistic**: You are not competing against anyone. You are doing this to fill your time in a positive way.
- **Focus on the Process**: Instead of worrying about perfect results, try to enjoy the act of learning. Even mistakes can be funny or interesting.
- **Use Beginner Resources**: Many classes, apps, or online videos cater to true beginners. Starting at the most basic level makes the first steps less scary.
- **Allow Yourself to Step Away**: If you truly dislike the new hobby, you can stop and try something else. There is no big risk in trying for a week or two.

Remind yourself that growth often comes with a bit of awkwardness at first. It is part of finding better ways to spend your free time.

11.9 Combining Routines and Hobbies

Your day can flow more smoothly if you build a routine that includes your hobbies. For instance:

1. **Morning Routine**: Wake up, drink a glass of water, do a quick stretch or gentle yoga, and then spend 15 minutes learning a language or playing an instrument before work.
2. **Afternoon Break**: If you have time off at midday, squeeze in a short hobby session—maybe reading a few pages of a book or tending to a small garden.
3. **Evening Routine**: Replace after-work drinks with a regular walk or a simple creative hobby. Try setting up an "art corner" or a "craft corner" at home where supplies are ready.
4. **Weekend Plans**: Join a local group or class on Saturdays or Sundays. Keep it consistent each week so it becomes a new habit.

When hobbies are woven into your routine, they become a normal part of your life, rather than an occasional extra.

11.10 Handling Boredom

At times, you might try a new routine or hobby but still feel bored. This can tempt you to return to alcohol for excitement or relief. To handle boredom:

- **Rotate Activities**: If you have three or four hobbies, you can switch between them to keep things fresh.
- **Invite Others**: Doing an activity with a friend can make it more lively. Even a simple home workout can be more fun with a partner.
- **Set Mini-Goals**: For example, if you are learning guitar, aim to learn one new chord per week. Reaching that target can give you a sense of progress.
- **Try a Challenge**: Many websites host short-term challenges, like writing a poem a day for a month or walking a certain number of steps each day. These can add spark to your routine.

Boredom often means you need variety or a bit of adventure. Adjust your plan as needed until you find a good balance.

11.11 Dealing with Lack of Motivation

You might have days when you do not feel like following your new routine. This is normal. Here are strategies to get moving:

- **Focus on Just Starting**: Promise yourself you will do the activity for only five minutes. Often, once you start, you will continue.
- **Remember Your Reasons**: You chose to quit alcohol to improve your life. Remind yourself that routines and hobbies support that.
- **Simplify the Steps**: If you planned a 30-minute exercise but feel too tired, at least do 5 or 10 minutes. It is better than skipping entirely.
- **Celebrate Small Milestones**: If you manage to follow your plan all week, treat yourself to a non-food or non-drink reward, like a small item for your hobby or a relaxing bath.

Motivation comes and goes. Build easy habits so you can keep going even when you are not feeling super excited.

11.12 The Impact on Emotional Health

Routines and hobbies can help stabilize your emotions. Alcohol once served as an escape or a quick way to change how you felt, but it also brought harm. Now, having a predictable schedule and fun activities offers:

- **A Healthy Stress Outlet**: Instead of getting worked up and turning to a drink, you have an alternative.
- **A Sense of Belonging**: If you join a social hobby group, you can feel part of a friendly circle. This lowers loneliness, which is a big trigger for some.
- **Improved Self-Esteem**: Learning or creating something new can make you feel proud, boosting your mood and self-respect.
- **Reduced Anxiety**: Knowing what your day will look like can reduce the fear of uncertainty. Unstructured time can lead to ruminating about problems.

As your emotional stability increases, cravings for alcohol tend to weaken because you are not seeking it to handle your feelings.

11.13 Time Management

When adding routines and hobbies, plan your day or week so you do not overstuff your schedule:

1. **Use a Planner or Calendar**: Write down your main obligations, then block out times for your new activities.
2. **Keep Realistic Gaps**: Leave some free space between tasks for rest, so you do not stress yourself trying to do too many things at once.
3. **Consider Your Peak Energy**: Some people have more energy in the morning, others in the evening. Place your more demanding hobby or routine at the time you feel best.
4. **Revisit Weekly**: At the end of each week, see how your schedule went. If it felt too packed, adjust. If it was too loose, add a bit more structure next time.

Good time management helps you stick to new habits without feeling overwhelmed.

11.14 Using Routines to Manage Triggers

Triggers can be times, places, or feelings that spark an urge to drink. Building routines around trigger points helps you stay safe:

- **Morning Anxiety**: If you used to handle stress by having a drink later in the day, set a morning routine that includes calming exercises or planning tasks. This can lower stress before it grows.
- **Post-Work Tiredness**: Many people want a drink right after work. If that is a trigger, plan a workout or a meet-up with a friend immediately after.
- **Weekend Evenings**: If Friday or Saturday nights were your main drinking times, schedule a movie night at home, a game night with friends who do not drink, or a relaxed bath-and-book routine.
- **Emotional Upsets**: If strong feelings like anger or sadness push you to drink, keep simple activities ready: walking, journaling, or calling a supportive friend.

Routines can act like a shield, directing you away from harmful impulses during vulnerable moments.

11.15 Adding Variety Over Time

As you get comfortable with your new ways of living, you may want to explore further:

- **Upgrade Existing Skills**: If you started with beginner guitar lessons, you could move to intermediate classes. If you have been walking for exercise, you might try short jogs.
- **Test a New Hobby**: Perhaps you mastered a simple craft and now want to try something else, like photography or cooking.
- **Expand Social Circles**: If you enjoy group activities, you could join a club that organizes weekend events or short trips.
- **Challenge Your Limits**: Sign up for a local 5K walk if you have been training. Or participate in an art fair if you have been painting. Small challenges keep you inspired.

There is no rush to pile on too many things, but gradual changes can keep life interesting and prevent boredom from returning.

CHAPTER 12: HANDLING SOCIAL SITUATIONS AND PEER PRESSURE

When you decide to quit or reduce drinking, social gatherings can feel like a big obstacle. Many events revolve around alcohol, from weekend parties to holiday dinners. Friends might tease you if you skip drinks. Family members might see it as rude if you refuse a toast. Coworkers might push after-work meetups at bars. All this can cause stress or temptation. But there are ways to stay strong and still have a good time.

In this chapter, we will go through a range of social settings, from parties to business events, and offer tips to keep your resolve. We will discuss the difference between real support and negative pressure. We will look at common remarks people make when you turn down a drink, and how to reply without feeling guilty. We will also explore how to plan for big gatherings and ways to navigate holiday traditions that focus on alcohol. By the end, you should feel more prepared to enjoy yourself while remaining loyal to your goals.

12.1 Recognizing Social Pressure

Social pressure is when people around you push you to act in a way you would rather not. It might be direct, like a friend saying, "Don't be boring—have a drink," or more subtle, like everyone at a table pouring wine except you. Humans like to fit in. If your group usually drinks, it can be hard to go against the flow.

Pressure can also be internal. You might feel you are missing out on fun if you do not drink. You might fear others think you are strange. Many times, though, this worry is bigger in our minds than in reality.

Examples of Social Pressure:

- Your old buddies invite you to a bar night and expect you to drink as usual.
- A family dinner where a relative says, "One little sip won't hurt you."
- A work event where the boss insists everyone toast with champagne.

Understanding that these moments can happen allows you to plan in advance. It is not about being rude or a killjoy. It is about protecting your progress.

12.2 Planning Before Events

A bit of planning can save you from stumbling under pressure:

1. **Know the Nature of the Event**: Is it a birthday party known for heavy drinking, or a casual get-together with mild social drinking? The level of alcohol focus helps you decide how cautious to be.
2. **Arrive Early or Late**: Sometimes arriving early lets you get settled and pick a non-alcoholic drink before others start pushing cocktails. Or coming a bit later might mean you skip the initial round of drinks.
3. **Bring a Friend**: If you have a supportive friend or partner who also avoids or limits alcohol, bring them. Having someone "on your team" reduces awkwardness.
4. **Set an End Time**: Plan how long you will stay. If it is a big party known to get wilder as the night goes on, you might leave before that happens.
5. **Visualize Your Responses**: Think about how you will turn down a drink if someone offers. Practicing your answers ahead of time keeps you from hesitating.

12.3 Simple Ways to Refuse Drinks

Turning down a drink does not require a long speech. Sometimes a short, confident answer works best:

- "No thanks, I'm good."
- "I'm focusing on my health, but thanks for asking."
- "I have an early morning tomorrow, so I'm sticking to something non-alcoholic."
- "I'm driving tonight, so I'm not drinking."

The key is to sound sure. If you act uncertain, people might push harder. A firm but friendly approach often ends the discussion. If someone insists, repeat your refusal once more and change the subject. If they still push, it says more about them than about you.

12.4 Handling Teasing or Criticism

Sometimes friends or family can tease or scold you for not joining in. They might say things like, "You used to be fun," or "Oh, so you think you're better than us?" This can hurt, especially if you care about their approval.

Ways to Handle Teasing:

1. **Stay Calm**: Responding with anger can escalate things. A calm reply, such as, "I'm just making a change for myself," can keep the tone neutral.
2. **Use Humor**: A light joke can deflect tension: "I'm fun enough without the hangover tomorrow!"
3. **Change the Topic**: If someone tries to argue, you can say, "Anyway, how have you been?" or bring up another subject.
4. **Exit the Scene**: If teasing does not stop, politely excuse yourself and move to another part of the room.

Over time, consistent behavior often quiets the teasing. People see you are serious and may back off.

12.5 Non-Alcoholic Drink Options

One issue at social events is what to hold in your hand if you are not drinking alcohol. Having a non-alcoholic drink can prevent people from asking, "Why aren't you drinking?" because they see you holding a glass.

Ideas for Non-Alcoholic Choices:

- Sparkling water with lime or lemon.
- Soft drinks (low-sugar if you prefer).
- Flavored teas or iced tea.
- Simple mocktails (juice with soda water and a garnish).
- Non-alcoholic beers or wines (some people find these helpful, while others prefer to avoid the taste of alcohol entirely).

Having a drink in hand can help you blend in and reduce questions about why you are not drinking.

12.6 Dealing with Holidays and Special Occasions

Holidays often come with traditions, like toasts of champagne or eggnog spiked with liquor. These can be hard to avoid. Yet you can still enjoy the festive mood without taking a drink.

1. **Plan Alternative Drinks**: For New Year's Eve, you might bring your own bottle of sparkling cider or non-alcoholic champagne so you can join the toast.
2. **Help with Food Prep**: If you are busy in the kitchen, you spend less time being offered drinks. Also, offering to be the person who hands out drinks can help you control what goes in your own glass.
3. **Stay Busy**: Be the one to organize games, music, or other fun things. This keeps you active and away from the drinks table.
4. **Offer to Drive**: If you drive others, you have a clear reason to not drink. Plus, you can leave when you are ready, limiting how long you are in a drinking environment.
5. **Pick the Right Seating**: If there is an option, sit by people who respect your choice or who also drink less. That lowers the pressure.

Holiday traditions might revolve around alcohol, but you can shape them to match your new lifestyle.

12.7 Business and Work Gatherings

Work-related events can feel tricky because you might worry about looking uncooperative if you do not join group drinks. However, you can still be social and professional without alcohol.

- **Keep a Professional Image**: Remember that getting drunk in front of coworkers or bosses can lead to problems. Many will respect your choice to stay clearheaded.
- **Network in Other Ways**: If the purpose is to mingle with clients or colleagues, focus on conversation rather than what is in your glass. Ask questions about their role or current projects.
- **Say You Are Driving**: This is often accepted in a work environment, as safety is a good reason not to drink.

- **Skip the After-Party**: If the official part ends and coworkers head to a bar, you can politely bow out if you sense it will turn into a drinking spree.
- **Choose a Non-Alcoholic Drink Early**: Arriving and ordering a soda water with lime or a soft drink right away sets the tone.

Being social does not require alcohol. You can still build relationships and show a friendly attitude.

12.8 Dealing with Old Drinking Buddies

If you had a circle of friends mainly connected by drinking, it can be tough to stay on track while seeing them. You might feel sad about missing old hangouts or worry that they will judge you. In some cases, you may need new social outlets. In other cases, you can remain friends if they respect your choice.

1. **Be Upfront**: Let them know you are serious about cutting back or stopping. If they cannot handle that, it might be time to limit contact.
2. **Suggest Other Activities**: If you used to meet only at bars, propose alternatives like watching a sports match at home with non-alcoholic snacks, or going to a coffee shop instead.
3. **Give Them Time**: Some friends adjust quickly. Others might need time to accept the "new you."
4. **Know Your Limits**: If you keep feeling pressured or uncomfortable, it might be best to step away for a while until you feel more stable.

Real friends should respect your decision. If they do not, ask if they really have your best interests at heart.

12.9 Telling People About Your Changes

When you stop drinking, people might notice. They could ask, "Why aren't you drinking tonight?" or "Have you stopped for good?" You do not owe anyone a deep explanation, but you can decide how much you want to share.

- **Simple Answers**: "I'm taking a break from alcohol," or "I decided it's better for my health."

- **Firm Tone**: If they keep asking, repeat your short answer or say, "I prefer not to talk about it right now," in a calm voice.
- **Positive Spin**: You can say, "I feel better this way," or "I have more energy without it." This might cut down on nosy questions.
- **Personal Choice**: If they press for details about past problems, you can say, "That's personal. I'm just making good changes."

Protect your privacy as needed. True friends will not push you to reveal more than you want.

12.10 Handling Events Where Alcohol Flows Freely

Some events, like weddings or music festivals, have lots of alcohol around. You can still have fun if you approach them wisely:

1. **Buddy System**: If you know someone else who is not drinking, plan to stick together. This can reduce temptation and help with awkward moments.
2. **Stay Hydrated**: Drinking plenty of water keeps your mind clear and can also give your hands something to hold.
3. **Focus on the Main Activity**: At a wedding, the focus is the couple's big day. At a festival, it is the music. Throw yourself into dancing, talking, or taking photos to capture the occasion.
4. **Set Boundaries**: If you feel overwhelmed, it is okay to step outside for fresh air or even leave earlier than others.
5. **Arrive with a Plan**: Know how you will respond if someone offers you a drink, and have a reason or polite refusal ready.

Large events can be busy and noisy, but you can shape your own experience in a positive, sober way.

12.11 Online Gatherings and Virtual Events

More and more social interactions happen online, including virtual parties or happy hours. It may be easier to skip a drink in these settings, but there can still be pressure if everyone else is showing off their wine or cocktails on camera.

- **Plan Your Beverage**: Have a cup of tea, flavored water, or a mocktail in a nice glass so you do not feel left out.
- **Short Attendance**: If it is not mandatory, you can stay just long enough to say hello and chat. Then sign off if the talk becomes all about drinking.
- **Change the Subject**: In an online call, it is easy to mention something else or ask a question about a person's day, job, or a shared interest. This can shift focus from "What are you drinking?"
- **Mute and Observe**: If the group is large, muting your microphone and just listening for a while can help you avoid direct pressure.

Online settings can be simpler in some ways, but it is still wise to have a plan for how to handle them.

12.12 Prioritizing Your Well-Being

When facing social pressure, the core point is to remember that your well-being is not up for debate. You have made a decision to quit or cut down. That is your right. People might pout, tease, or try to push you, but your health and goals matter more than their opinions.

- **Self-Respect**: Say to yourself, "I have the right to protect my progress."
- **Confidence**: Walk into social events with your head high. If you look uneasy, others might sense it and challenge you more.
- **Escape Plans**: If you ever feel cornered, you can leave. That is not weakness. It is self-care.
- **Balance**: Many people discover that they still can laugh, dance, and share good memories without a drop of alcohol.

Over time, you might find a new circle that does not focus on heavy drinking. Or your current social circle might adapt to your changes. In either case, you will see that it is possible to have a busy, satisfying social life while sticking to your alcohol-free goal.

CHAPTER 13: LONG-TERM HEALTH CHECKS AND BODY CHANGES

When you stop or greatly reduce drinking, the positive changes do not end after the first few weeks. In fact, many benefits appear gradually over months or even years. Your body has a way of healing if given the right support—nutrition, rest, and time. You might have seen short-term gains, like reduced hangovers and better sleep. But long-term improvements can be even more significant.

In this chapter, we will look at what can happen physically and mentally in the months and years after quitting or cutting down on alcohol. We will explore how regular checkups with health professionals can spot improvements or catch any ongoing issues. We will go through shifts in liver health, heart health, brain function, and more. We will also talk about how to track these changes at home, such as keeping an eye on vital signs or using simple devices. By learning about this bigger picture, you can see that your decision to quit has benefits that keep unfolding.

13.1 The Body's Ability to Recover

The human body is resilient. Even if you have been a heavy drinker for many years, once you cut out or reduce alcohol, your cells can start repairing themselves. The speed and extent of recovery depends on how severe the damage was, plus factors like age, genetics, and overall lifestyle.

- **Liver Regeneration**: The liver is the main organ that processes toxins like alcohol. If damage was not too advanced, liver cells can renew.
- **Brain Plasticity**: The brain can adapt and restore some functions that were dulled by alcohol. Memory, focus, and emotional regulation can improve.
- **Immune System Strength**: Chronic drinking weakens your immune system. Once you stop, you may notice you get fewer colds or infections.
- **Energy Boost**: Your body is no longer dealing with the depressant effects of alcohol or the ups and downs of blood sugar spikes.

While not all damage is reversible, it is surprising how much the body can bounce back. Regular health checkups help you see these improvements clearly.

13.2 Scheduling Medical Checkups

After you stop drinking, it is wise to see your doctor for a thorough exam. This might include:

1. **Blood Tests**: They can measure liver enzymes, blood sugar, and other markers. Seeing them improve over time can be inspiring.
2. **Blood Pressure Checks**: Heavy drinking often raises blood pressure. Once you reduce or quit, you might see it go down.
3. **Nutrient Levels**: Long-term drinkers can be low in B vitamins, vitamin D, magnesium, and other nutrients. Tests can check for deficiencies.
4. **Mental Health Evaluation**: If you have felt anxious or sad, discussing it with a professional can help them see if things are improving or need extra support.

Try to schedule these visits regularly—maybe every six months or year. This pattern lets you track the gradual impact of your new lifestyle.

13.3 Changes in Liver Health

The liver can face fatty buildup and inflammation after years of heavy drinking. Stopping alcohol gives the liver a chance to recover.

- **Fatty Liver Reversal**: In early stages, the liver can clear out excess fat once alcohol is removed. This might take a few weeks to months.
- **Reduced Inflammation**: If there was mild hepatitis, quitting alcohol helps calm the inflammation.
- **Lower Cirrhosis Risk**: Cirrhosis involves permanent scarring. If you already have cirrhosis, stopping further damage is crucial to avoid complications.
- **Regular Scans**: In some cases, a doctor might do an ultrasound or other imaging to watch your liver's condition over time.

Not everyone with liver damage returns to fully normal function. But many see major improvements in lab results and fewer symptoms, like fatigue or discomfort.

13.4 Heart and Circulation Benefits

Alcohol can harm the heart by raising blood pressure and impacting how the heart muscle works. Over time, heavy drinking boosts the risk of heart problems. Once you stop, the body can shift toward healthier patterns.

- **Blood Pressure Drop**: Elevated blood pressure often responds within weeks or months of cutting out alcohol. This can reduce the risk of stroke and heart disease.
- **Heart Rhythm**: Some people experience irregular heartbeats (arrhythmias) linked to drinking. This might improve once alcohol is out of the picture.
- **Cholesterol and Triglycerides**: Alcohol can alter these levels in harmful ways. Stopping may help bring them back to a better range, especially when paired with good nutrition.
- **Better Circulation**: Fewer episodes of flushing, racing heart, or cold extremities.

Staying active and eating well can further boost heart health. Regular checkups help your doctor note if medications or other treatments might help you too.

13.5 Brain and Cognitive Improvements

Chronic alcohol use can affect memory, decision-making, and mental clarity. Quitting often leads to slow but steady gains in mental function.

- **Clearer Thinking**: You might notice you remember tasks better, solve problems faster, or have more mental stamina.
- **Better Mood Regulation**: Alcohol can create mood swings. Without it, your brain can balance chemicals that affect happiness and calmness.
- **Reduced Brain Shrinkage**: Research shows heavy drinking can shrink certain brain areas. Stopping might prevent further shrinkage and let some functions bounce back.
- **Improved Sleep Quality**: Although you might have trouble at first, over the long run, stable sleep cycles help your mind recharge.

Some changes might be subtle at first, but friends or family might notice your increased alertness and better reactions.

13.6 Weight and Metabolism Shifts

Alcohol is high in empty calories. Many people notice they start losing weight once they quit, or they find it easier to maintain a healthy weight.

- **Lower Calorie Intake**: Removing daily drinks can cut hundreds of calories.
- **Reduced Cravings**: Some who quit alcohol stop craving sugary foods as strongly, as their body's balance returns to normal.
- **More Room for Nutritious Foods**: If you used to fill up on alcohol, now you can eat balanced meals that support metabolism.
- **Steadier Blood Sugar**: Alcohol can spike and crash blood sugar, leaving you hungry or shaky. Without it, you might have more consistent energy levels.

Keep in mind, some people replace alcohol with sugary snacks at first. Watch your diet to avoid just swapping one habit for another.

13.7 Skin and Appearance

Drinking can cause dehydration and harm the skin's appearance. With time away from alcohol, you might notice:

- **Brighter Complexion**: Less puffiness or redness, especially around the face.
- **Fewer Blemishes**: Alcohol can worsen breakouts by messing with hormone levels and hydration.
- **Reduced Dark Circles**: Better sleep and hydration can lessen under-eye darkness.
- **Healthier Hair**: Drinking less can boost nutrient absorption, which may lead to shinier hair.

Small details like these can increase self-confidence. Noticing physical improvements can encourage you to keep going.

13.8 Emotional Stability and Stress Response

In the first few weeks, emotions can be rocky as the body and mind adjust. Over the longer term, though, most people find they handle stress better without alcohol in the picture.

- **Stronger Coping Skills**: Since you are no longer using alcohol to mask troubles, you develop real problem-solving strategies.
- **Reduced Anxiety or Anger Outbursts**: Alcohol can amplify negative moods. Without it, you might feel calmer day to day.
- **Better Self-Esteem**: Feeling proud of sticking to your plan can boost how you see yourself. This good feeling can spread to other parts of life, like work or relationships.
- **Healthier Relationships**: Reduced arguments, more honest communication, and being truly present can help rebuild trust with loved ones.

Professional support, like therapy, can speed up this emotional growth. But even on your own, time away from drinking often reveals a more stable mood pattern.

13.9 Tracking Progress at Home

Aside from doctor visits, you can keep an eye on your health at home:

1. **Blood Pressure Cuff**: An affordable device lets you measure your pressure weekly. Watching it drop can be motivating.
2. **Weight Scale**: Weighing yourself once a week can show if you are steadily losing or maintaining a healthier weight.
3. **Sleep Diary**: Jot down how many hours you slept and how rested you felt upon waking. Over time, you might see real improvement.
4. **Mood Journal**: Mark each day with a quick note on your mood. Patterns might emerge, showing fewer down days.
5. **Symptom Notes**: If you had any physical discomfort when you drank (like stomach pain), you can note if it goes away.

This home tracking does not replace professional checkups, but it can keep you engaged in the process.

13.10 Watching Out for Hidden Issues

Sometimes, quitting alcohol can reveal or heighten underlying issues, such as depression or chronic pain. When you drank, the alcohol might have dulled certain signals. Now that you are sober, you might notice these problems more.

- **Chronic Conditions**: You might realize you have a back problem or stomach issue that was masked by frequent drinking.
- **Emotional Trauma**: Past events that you tried to bury with alcohol could come to the surface, requiring counseling.
- **Social Anxiety**: Some people used alcohol as "liquid courage" in crowds. Without it, you might need new coping tools.

Try not to see these discoveries as setbacks. It is better to know what is really going on, so you can address it properly. Therapists, doctors, or support groups can help you tackle these hidden issues.

13.11 Staying Motivated During Slow Progress

Long-term healing can be slow. Some changes, like lowering liver enzyme levels, might happen fairly quickly, but others—like reversing certain nerve problems—can take a long time. You might have plateaus where nothing seems to improve. This is normal.

Ways to Stay Motivated:

1. **Mark Small Wins**: If your blood pressure improved slightly or you slept better a few nights in a row, acknowledge that.
2. **Review Before/After**: Look back at how you felt or your lab results six months ago versus now. That perspective can show real progress.
3. **Set Non-Health Goals**: Maybe you focus on a fitness milestone or a new hobby. Achieving these can keep you excited.
4. **Use Support Systems**: Share your progress with friends, a counselor, or online groups. They can remind you of how far you have come.

Remember that your body took time to adjust to heavy drinking. It also takes time to return to a healthier state.

13.12 Looking to the Future

As you move deeper into an alcohol-free or reduced-alcohol life, your sense of normal changes. You wake up feeling clear-headed. You handle stress with real coping methods. You plan for social events without fear. You might even find new passions or realize your relationships are stronger than ever.

Long-term, you can keep up regular checkups and watch for any signs of relapse. But overall, life becomes about more than "not drinking." It becomes about living in a balanced way, taking care of your body and mind, and discovering what you can do now that you are not held back by alcohol. Some people decide to get involved in helping others who are starting to quit. Others invest energy into fitness, career, or family. The path forward is wide open.

CHAPTER 14: SPOTTING WARNING SIGNS OF PROBLEMS

After working hard to quit or reduce alcohol, it can feel like you have passed the toughest part. However, unexpected problems or hidden threats can appear at any time. These problems might not always be about returning to heavy drinking. They could be physical, emotional, or social issues that weaken your resolve if you do not catch them early. The key is to know what to look for before a small issue grows bigger.

In this chapter, we will explore the warning signs that indicate a risk of returning to old habits, developing a new unhealthy pattern, or facing emotional troubles that can open the door to drinking again. We will talk about how these signs can appear in your body, your mental state, and your relationships. We will also look at actions to take if you notice them, such as reviewing your strategies, seeking outside help, or changing routines. By staying aware of potential pitfalls, you can fix small cracks in your plan and stay on track.

14.1 Small Slips vs. Full Setbacks

One important part of spotting warning signs is knowing the difference between a small slip and a full-blown setback. A slip might be a one-time event or a brief moment of returning to old behavior. You might drink a glass of wine under social pressure or feel an unexpected craving and cave in for one evening. While this is not good, you can recover quickly with the right steps. A full setback is a longer return to heavy use or total neglect of your healthy habits.

Clues That a Slip Is Approaching

- You catch yourself frequently daydreaming about the "good sides" of drinking.
- You start pushing away your support system, skipping check-ins or group meetings.
- You find reasons to be around drinking environments, telling yourself you just want to "test" your willpower.
- You notice your stress level is sky-high, and you are not using any healthy coping methods.

Why This Matters

Recognizing the signs of a slip early allows you to pause and correct your course before it becomes a complete relapse. A small slip is easier to manage if you treat it seriously, rather than hiding it or pretending it did not happen.

14.2 Physical Warning Signs

The body can give signals that something is off. Being attuned to these clues can help you stop a slide toward negative outcomes:

1. **Changes in Sleep Patterns**: If you suddenly find it hard to fall asleep or stay asleep, it might mean you are stressed. Poor sleep can lower your resolve and lead to cravings for a "quick fix."
2. **Unusual Fatigue or Low Energy**: Constant tiredness might suggest you are not eating properly, ignoring exercise, or facing emotional strain. If you used to feel more energetic after quitting alcohol and now feel sluggish again, it is worth looking at what changed.
3. **Unsteady Mood Swings**: If your body chemistry is out of balance, you might experience physical signs like shakiness, faster heartbeat, or sweating when anxious. These can sometimes mimic the feelings you had during withdrawal.
4. **Headaches or Stomach Issues**: Stress and anxiety often show up as tension headaches or digestive problems. These might drive you to seek relief in old habits if you are not careful.
5. **Sudden Cravings for Sugary Foods**: Some people replace alcohol with sugary snacks or drinks. If you notice you are going overboard with candy or desserts, it might be a clue that you are unconsciously trying to fill the void alcohol left.

When these physical signs show up, do a quick review of your habits: Are you skipping meals? Are you neglecting exercise? Are you pushing yourself too hard at work?

14.3 Emotional and Mental Red Flags

Feelings are powerful. Many people drink to handle sadness, frustration, or worry. Keep an eye on these emotional signals:

1. **Irritability or Anger Spikes**: If small things make you unusually angry, it might suggest unaddressed stress building up. In the past, you might have used alcohol to calm this anger. Now, you need other methods.
2. **Constant Anxiety**: Mild nervousness is common, but if you feel trapped in a cycle of worry all day, it could weaken your resolve.
3. **Feeling Numb or Empty**: Sometimes, if you have lost the excitement of life without finding healthy replacements, you might feel empty. This emptiness can push you to crave the "rush" from alcohol.
4. **Unmanaged Grief or Sadness**: Past losses or current struggles can reappear without warning. If you have not dealt with them properly, they can push you toward old solutions.
5. **Restlessness or Boredom**: Doing better with alcohol does not guarantee you feel fulfilled. If your days seem dull, you might start longing for the old "buzz" just to break the boredom.

If you spot these emotional red flags, it might be time to talk to a counselor, revisit coping strategies, or increase your engagement with social support.

14.4 Social Warning Signs

Those around you can shape how you view drinking. Notice if your social world is shifting in ways that raise your risk:

1. **Spending Time with Heavier Drinkers Again**: If old friends who still drink heavily start to reappear, or if you begin seeking them out, you might be edging toward unsafe territory.
2. **Avoiding Supportive People**: If you are deliberately not returning calls or skipping hangouts with friends who respect your new lifestyle, you might be moving away from accountability.
3. **Keeping Secrets**: If you catch yourself lying about where you go or what you do, it can be a sign of shame or hidden behavior. Dishonesty can speed up a slide toward relapse.
4. **Frequent Party Invites**: Sometimes, social groups might push you to attend gatherings full of alcohol. If you find yourself saying "yes" when you used to set boundaries, it might indicate a problem.
5. **Arguments or Tension at Home**: Stressful relationships with close family or a partner can spark emotional pressure that leads to craving a drink.

Keep tabs on how your social circle behaves and how you respond. It is not about avoiding all social contact, but about keeping an eye on changes in how you spend your time and with whom.

14.5 Warning Signs at Work or School

Job or academic environments can become high-pressure zones. If you have too much stress, lack of structure, or conflicts with colleagues or classmates, it might trigger old coping behaviors:

1. **Sudden Drop in Performance**: Missing deadlines, making repeated mistakes, or feeling unable to concentrate could be stress indicators.
2. **Frequent Urge to Escape After Work**: If you are constantly counting down the minutes to "happy hour," it might hint you are slipping into the old mindset that you need a drink to unwind.
3. **Increased Absences**: Feeling drained or unmotivated might lead you to skip work or classes more often. This can further raise stress and the temptation to self-medicate.
4. **Arguments or Conflicts with Supervisors**: If your patience is short and you are clashing with higher-ups, you might end your day feeling angry or hopeless, which can feed cravings.
5. **Isolation**: Hiding at your desk, avoiding group projects, or refusing social invites (even sober ones) can signal that you are pulling away. Isolation weakens your safety net.

If these appear, talk with a counselor at work or school. They can help you manage the stress more productively.

14.6 Financial Red Flags

When you quit alcohol, you might see your finances improve because you are not spending on drinks. But financial pressure can rise from other angles:

- **Impulse Shopping**: Some people replace alcohol with online shopping or other spending. Watch for unplanned purchases that strain your budget and create stress.

- **Money Arguments**: If you share finances with a partner, conflicts over money might reflect deeper tension or a new stressor that tempts you to escape.
- **Late Bills**: If you lose track of bills or ignore them because of anxiety, it can snowball and add more stress to your life.
- **Gambling**: A few individuals swap drinking for gambling. This might appear harmless at first but can lead to major financial trouble.
- **Stalled Career Growth**: Maybe you are not investing in your own training or education. Feeling stuck can add frustration, making you think about a "quick solution."

Keep finances organized. A monthly budget review might reveal if you are picking up an unhealthy habit or ignoring problems that could push you back toward alcohol as a coping method.

14.7 Warning Signs in Routine and Self-Care

Routine and self-care are pillars of staying away from alcohol. If you see them weakening, it can hint at trouble:

1. **Skipping Meals**: You might revert to poor eating habits, whether through snacking on junk or missing meals altogether. This can throw off your mood and energy.
2. **Dropping Exercise**: If you used to walk or do light workouts and now you never make time, you lose a major stress reliever.
3. **Ignoring Personal Grooming**: If you stop caring about cleanliness or your appearance, it might mean you feel low or discouraged.
4. **Chaotic Sleep Patterns**: Staying up too late, sleeping too little, or oversleeping can affect mental stability.
5. **Not Taking Breaks**: Working non-stop or never pausing for mental rest can deplete you, leaving you vulnerable to old habits.

Think about your daily and weekly schedule. If key pieces of self-care vanish, it is time to ask why and correct course.

14.8 Mental Health Concerns

If you had underlying mental health issues (like sadness or anxiety disorders), they might flare up again in times of stress. Or perhaps you never realized you had them because alcohol masked symptoms. Warning signs can include:

1. **Lingering Gloom**: Feeling sad, hopeless, or uninterested in things you used to like for several weeks.
2. **Panic Spikes**: Frequent panic attacks or consistent dread about everyday tasks.
3. **Loss of Pleasure**: Nothing seems fun or meaningful, which can push you to think about using alcohol for excitement.
4. **Thoughts of Giving Up**: If you catch yourself thinking life is too hard or you want to quit trying, this signals a need for immediate help.
5. **Trouble Leaving the House**: Isolation or fear of social settings can grow if not addressed.

In these cases, professional counseling or therapy is often the best route. There is no shame in seeking help to protect your progress and well-being.

14.9 Behavioral Clues from Loved Ones

Sometimes, loved ones notice warning signs before you do. They might see changes in your mood, routine, or communication style that you miss. If friends, family, or a partner brings up concerns, listen carefully:

- They mention you seem distant or edgy.
- They worry about you returning to old patterns.
- They see you avoiding social contact.
- They notice you are increasingly defensive or sensitive about simple questions.
- They point out changes in your daily habits, like skipping showers or forgetting errands.

It can be hard to hear such feedback, but often they are trying to help. Instead of pushing them away, consider if there is truth in what they say.

14.10 Spiritual or Personal Values

Not everyone connects their lifestyle with spiritual or personal values, but for some, these can be significant. If you once found strength in a set of beliefs or moral guidelines and now feel you are drifting away, that sense of loss might open a path back to alcohol.

- **Conflict with Beliefs**: If you are doing things that clash with your values (like lying to loved ones), you might feel guilt, which can trigger cravings.
- **Lack of Purpose**: Feeling that life lacks meaning can lead you to seek a quick "high" or escape.
- **Quitting Involvement**: If you used to attend faith gatherings or do volunteer work and suddenly stop, you could be losing a source of support.

Staying connected to what motivates you or gives you purpose can anchor your commitment to an alcohol-free life.

14.11 Recognizing Cross-Addiction Risks

Sometimes, people who quit alcohol shift to another addictive habit. This can include gambling, drugs, or even compulsive use of social media. Warning signs of cross-addiction include:

1. **Needing More of the New Habit**: You start with moderate behavior (maybe a little online shopping) but quickly it grows excessive.
2. **Hiding the New Habit**: You feel guilty or do it in secret, like waiting until everyone sleeps to binge on something.
3. **Using It to Cope**: Similar to alcohol, you turn to the new behavior whenever stressed or upset.
4. **Financial or Social Damage**: This new activity starts affecting your job, relationships, or bank balance.
5. **Same Emotional Patterns**: You notice the same cycle: tension builds, you act on the new habit, then feel a short relief followed by regret.

If this is happening, it is vital to get help before you swap one harmful habit for another.

14.12 Communication Patterns That Show Danger

The way you talk to yourself and others can also hold warnings:

- **Making Excuses**: You find reasons for skipping accountability steps, like, "I'm too busy for therapy this week," or, "I can handle it alone."
- **Being Defensive**: If any mention of your habits leads you to lash out or deny there is a problem, you might be in denial.
- **Rationalizing**: You might say, "I only had two drinks; it's not like before." But if those two drinks were a slip from your plan, it matters.
- **Blaming**: Shifting blame onto others, like, "I wouldn't feel this way if my boss wasn't so demanding," or "My spouse caused me to slip."
- **Belittling Your Progress**: Downplaying your own success can lower your self-esteem, making you more likely to consider drinking again.

Communication is both internal (self-talk) and external (how you speak to others). If it becomes negative or filled with denial, you are at risk.

14.13 Handling Early Indicators Once You Spot Them

So, what do you do if you catch these warning signs?

1. **Acknowledge Them**: First, accept that the sign is real. Denial only gives it time to grow.
2. **Review Your Strategies**: Revisit the coping methods or routines that worked for you at the start. Are you still doing them, or have you let them slip?
3. **Talk About It**: Speak with a friend, counselor, or group about what you have noticed. Fresh perspectives can guide you back on track.
4. **Strengthen Boundaries**: If you see social or work environments causing issues, re-establish your limits. That might mean saying "no" to certain invites or tasks.
5. **Address Underlying Problems**: If you find that your sadness or job stress is fueling cravings, consider therapy or changes in your life, such as seeking a new role or adjusting your workload.

The earlier you act, the easier it is to correct your path and avoid bigger fallout.

14.14 Tools for Self-Monitoring

Practical tools can help you spot and address warning signs:

- **Daily Mood Tracker**: Rate your mood each day on a scale. A sudden dip might hint at new stressors.
- **Cravings Log**: Note the time, place, and reason you felt an urge. Look for patterns like "every time I argue with my partner" or "every Friday after work."
- **Checklist of Habits**: Make a simple chart of tasks you consider vital: healthy meals, exercise, journaling, bedtime. Mark which ones you do. If you see too many unchecked boxes, that's a sign.
- **Regular Support Calls**: Schedule a weekly call with a friend or mentor specifically to discuss how you are feeling.
- **Professional Check-Ins**: If you can, book periodic sessions with a counselor. They can pick up on warning signs you may overlook.

These tools create structure and keep you informed about shifts in your well-being.

14.15 Responses to Loved Ones' Concerns

Sometimes, warning signs become visible to family or friends before you notice them. If they raise a concern:

- **Pause and Listen**: Fight the urge to snap back defensively. Hear them out.
- **Ask for Specifics**: "What changes have you noticed?" This can reveal blind spots.
- **Appreciate Their Input**: You might say, "I'm glad you told me. I want to stay on track."
- **Invite Solutions**: Ask how they might support you. Maybe they can help watch for triggers or join you in healthy activities.
- **Avoid Shutting Down**: Even if the talk feels uncomfortable, it is better to face it now than let a small problem become bigger.

Good communication can turn an awkward conversation into a helpful intervention that saves you from a serious slip.

14.16 Partner or Family Arguments

Conflicts at home can be a huge driver of stress. Warning signs here include repeated arguments, tense silences, or feeling that you cannot talk about your concerns. Some suggestions:

1. **Calm Talking**: Pick a time when both sides are less emotional. Talk calmly about the problems.
2. **Seek Mediation**: A counselor or neutral third party can help you communicate better, preventing fights that might drive you toward old habits.
3. **Own Your Role**: If you have been irritable or distant, recognize it. This honesty can reduce tension.
4. **Set Time-Outs**: If a conversation heats up, agree to pause and return once you both cool off. This prevents saying hurtful words that add fuel to the fire.
5. **Unified Goals**: Work together on stress management or finances if those are the sources of conflict. Teamwork can reduce anger and blame.

A stable home environment is a major defense against cravings, so spotting conflict is crucial.

14.17 Work-Related Anxiety

If your job or career is the main cause of stress, watch for signs like dreading each day, trouble focusing, or losing interest in tasks you used to find meaningful. A few solutions:

- **Chat with HR or a Mentor**: Sometimes, a small change in duties or schedule helps.
- **Plan Career Moves**: If your job truly overwhelms you, explore new roles or training that can lead to a less stressful position.
- **Set Work Boundaries**: Avoid answering work emails all night if possible. Overwork can sap your energy.
- **Short Breaks**: Even a quick walk outside at lunch can reset your mind.
- **Therapy for Work Stress**: A professional can give strategies to manage conflicts with coworkers or workload pressures.

Being proactive can block the cycle of frustration that leads to old coping methods.

14.18 Advanced Warning: Feeling Overly Confident

Interestingly, feeling too confident can also be a danger. After a few months or years of success, you might think you are fully safe. Signs of overconfidence include:

- **Dropping All Checks**: You stop journaling or talking to your support system because you believe you do not need them.
- **Testing Yourself**: You place yourself in tempting situations for the thrill of proving you can resist.
- **Mocking Others' Warnings**: If friends or family gently caution you and you brush them off as worrying too much.
- **Feeling Invincible**: You start believing you can "handle just one drink," ignoring the lessons of the past.
- **Neglecting Health**: You might stop healthy habits, thinking you have everything figured out.

It is good to feel proud of your progress, but never forget how powerful addiction can be. A balanced attitude is the safest path.

14.19 Community or Group Warning Signs

If you are part of a support group or an online community, pay attention to the atmosphere there:

- **Negative Shifts**: If group members often talk about giving up or share harmful tips, it might drag you down.
- **Loss of Moderation**: In online groups without good moderation, trolls or spam can create a toxic mood.
- **Ignoring Accountability**: If the group stops holding each other accountable, you might lose a vital safety net.
- **Unhelpful Comparisons**: Some people might brag about how quickly they quit, making you feel behind or discouraged. This can undermine your self-esteem.
- **Group Conflicts**: Frequent arguments or "cliques" forming might make the group less safe as a support space.

If you notice these signs, consider finding a healthier support network or bringing it up to the group's leaders.

CHAPTER 15: HELPING OTHERS AND SHARING ADVICE

One of the most fulfilling ways to strengthen your own progress is to help others who struggle with alcohol. You might not be a certified counselor or health professional, but your personal experience can still be a source of hope for friends, family, coworkers, or even strangers online. When you share what you have learned, you remind yourself of the reasons you quit or cut down. You also spread helpful information that might save someone else from years of difficulty.

This chapter covers how to approach people who are facing similar challenges, how to give practical tips without overstepping, and how to protect your own well-being in the process. We will discuss the difference between being supportive and trying to fix someone else's life. We will also look at ways to show empathy, create a safe environment for honest talk, and possibly guide them toward professional help. By the end, you should have a clearer sense of how to encourage others while keeping your own progress strong.

15.1 Reasons to Help Others

Reaching a place where you feel stable with your own drinking habits is a big step. Helping others can:

1. **Keep Your Motivation High**: Reminding yourself of what you overcame can stop you from sliding back.
2. **Build a Sense of Purpose**: Knowing you made someone's day better or eased their fears can boost self-esteem.
3. **Strengthen Your Skills**: Teaching others about healthy routines or coping methods refines your own understanding.
4. **Create Community**: You might find new friendships or support networks by being the one who listens and shares.
5. **Pay Forward the Support**: If mentors, friends, or a program helped you, you can pass on that kindness to someone else.

15.2 Deciding How Involved to Get

There is a difference between being a friendly ear and becoming someone's sole supporter. You want to help, but you also need to protect your own progress. Consider:

- **Time and Energy**: Helping someone might mean phone calls, texts, or meetups. Make sure you have the capacity to be there for them without ignoring your needs.
- **Your Emotional Boundaries**: If their struggles trigger your own cravings, you might need to step back or guide them to a different source of help.
- **Nature of Your Relationship**: Is this a close friend, a family member, or a distant acquaintance? If it is someone you barely know, your approach might be more limited.
- **Professional Backup**: If the person needs therapy or medical help, encourage them to seek it. You can be a support, but not a replacement for expert care.

Balancing your own well-being with the desire to help is crucial. Overextending can harm both of you.

15.3 Recognizing the Right Moment to Offer Help

You might see a friend complaining about hangovers, missing work, or running into relationship trouble due to drinking. It is natural to want to step in. But timing matters:

- **Check Their Mood**: If they are defensive or angry, they might reject any suggestions.
- **Pick a Calm Setting**: Bringing up personal issues in a crowded room or busy time often leads to resistance.
- **Look for Openings**: If they mention feeling stuck or wanting a change, that is your chance to say, "I've gone through something similar—are you open to ideas?"
- **Avoid Public Lectures**: Calling someone out in front of others might embarrass them. Private chats can be more productive.

Your role is not to force them to see a problem, but to open the door so they know help is available.

15.4 Sharing Your Own Experience

Your story can be powerful, but how you share it makes a difference:

1. **Focus on Honesty**: Mention the struggles you faced, the steps that helped you, and what you learned. Avoid exaggerating or pretending it was easier or harder than it was.
2. **Keep It Brief**: You do not need to recount every detail. People might only need to know that you have been there and found a path forward.
3. **Highlight Practical Tips**: For instance, mention how you used a daily routine, found support groups, or handled cravings. This shows them doable actions.
4. **Avoid Preaching**: Offer your insights, but do not order them to follow your exact plan. Everyone's path can vary.
5. **Stay Respectful**: They might still be in a different stage of readiness. If they shut down, do not push too hard. Let them know you are around if they want to talk later.

Sharing experiences with empathy and respect often resonates more than giving a list of instructions.

15.5 Providing Practical Advice

When someone asks for concrete help, you can share steps that worked for you or that you have learned from reliable sources:

- **Suggest Simple Routines**: Outline how having set meal times or bedtime schedules can stabilize their day.
- **Recommend Support Options**: Give them contact information for local help lines, online forums, or counseling services.
- **Mention Helpful Books or Tools**: If certain books, trackers, or apps helped you track cravings or manage stress, let them know.
- **Discuss Setting Goals**: Encourage them to pick small, clear targets, like staying alcohol-free on weekdays or logging each drink in a diary.
- **Explain Basic Self-Care**: Talk about the importance of hydration, nutrition, and mild exercise for mood balance.

Keep the advice actionable and easy to understand. Overloading them with complex plans might discourage them from starting.

15.6 Being a Supportive Listener

Sometimes, people do not want advice right away. They might just want someone to hear their frustrations:

1. **Use Active Listening**: Give them your full attention. Nod or say short phrases like, "That sounds tough," or, "I understand."
2. **Avoid Quick Fixes**: Let them finish talking before jumping in with solutions. They might just need to vent.
3. **Ask Open-Ended Questions**: "How did you feel at that moment?" or "What worries you the most?" This shows you care about their experience.
4. **Reflect Back**: Summarize what they said to confirm understanding: "You feel overwhelmed because of work and family stress, and you turn to alcohol to cope. Is that right?"
5. **Offer Empathy, Not Judgment**: Show you understand it is hard. Judging them can make them defensive or ashamed.

Being a patient listener can build trust. Once trust is there, they may be more open to trying new ideas.

15.7 Avoiding Common Pitfalls

Even with good intentions, you can make mistakes. Here are some missteps:

- **Pushing Too Hard**: Repeating your advice too many times can make them withdraw.
- **Guilt-Tripping**: Saying, "Think of how you're hurting everyone!" can create shame rather than motivation.
- **Taking On Their Problems**: You are not responsible for solving every aspect of their life. Maintain boundaries.
- **Comparing Trauma**: Telling them, "Your situation isn't as bad as mine was," can minimize their feelings.
- **Making Promises You Cannot Keep**: If you say you will always be available 24/7 but then cannot handle the late-night calls, it erodes trust.

Sticking to realistic, respectful support keeps the relationship healthy.

15.8 Encouraging Professional Help

If someone's alcohol use is severe or they have underlying health or mental issues, they may need professional intervention:

1. **Explain the Benefits**: Mention how doctors, therapists, or rehab programs can create a safer plan, especially if they have physical dependence.
2. **Dispel Myths**: Some fear seeking help because they think it is too expensive, too strict, or too shameful. Share facts if you know them.
3. **Offer to Go with Them**: If you are close, you might say, "I can accompany you to the appointment if you want support."
4. **Give Options**: Provide phone numbers of local help lines, or websites that list treatment centers. If they sense they have choices, they might be less resistant.
5. **Respect Their Timing**: If they refuse right now, do not force them. Keep the door open in case they change their mind.

Professional help can be a turning point, but the person has to decide they are ready.

15.9 Creating a Positive Environment

If you live with or frequently see the person you are helping, think about how your shared space or activities can support healthier habits:

- **Keep Alcohol Out of Sight**: If you are both trying to reduce or avoid it, do not store bottles in the living room or on countertops.
- **Suggest Fun Alternatives**: Plan outings that do not revolve around bars—like visiting a park, game nights, or movie nights with non-alcoholic drinks.
- **Celebrate Milestones in a Healthy Way**: If they reach a target like a sober week, mark the moment with something enjoyable (like cooking a nice meal or playing a board game).
- **Offer Small Routines Together**: A morning walk or a light workout can form a supportive routine.
- **Kind Reminders**: If you see them feeling shaky, you can say, "Remember how good you felt last week without drinking. Want to talk about what's bothering you?"

These shifts can make a big difference in how they handle cravings day to day.

15.10 Online Support and Social Media

Some people might not have strong in-person networks but find support online. You can still help:

- **Forums or Groups**: If you are part of a sober living group or chat, you can message them, answer their questions, or share links to resources.
- **Moderate Tone**: Written text can be misunderstood. Keep a calm, friendly tone to avoid arguments.
- **Encourage Safe Spaces**: If the person faces toxic comments on some platforms, suggest they switch to a more positive group.
- **Share Articles or Videos**: Linking to reliable information can guide them to read at their own pace.
- **Check In Regularly**: Online contact can be quick. Even a short daily message can help them feel less alone.

The internet can provide quick help 24/7, but remind them to verify health facts with professionals if it is a serious concern.

15.11 Handling Resistance or Rejection

Not everyone will accept your help. They might deny they have a problem, push you away, or say hurtful things. This is difficult, especially if you care about them:

1. **Stay Patient**: Sometimes, people need to process the idea of change on their own schedule.
2. **Avoid Arguing**: Trying to force your point when they are defensive can lock them into denial.
3. **Maintain Warmth**: Let them know you are still there if they decide they want help. "I respect your choice. If you ever want to talk, I'm here."
4. **Protect Your Emotions**: It can be painful to watch someone struggle. Seek your own support if you feel discouraged or guilty.
5. **Recognize Limits**: If their behavior is toxic or harmful, you might have to set strong boundaries for your own safety.

Sometimes, the best you can do is plant a seed. They might come back to you in the future when they are ready.

15.12 Teaching by Example

Words matter, but actions can be more convincing. If people see you living well without alcohol and handling stress in healthier ways, they might feel inspired:

- **Show Balance**: Demonstrate that you manage stress through hobbies, social contacts, or mild exercise instead of escaping into a substance.
- **Stay Consistent**: If you used to drink heavily, your new habits can speak loudly to those who knew the "old you."
- **Own Up to Slip-Ups**: If you do have a slip, be open about how you handled it. This honesty can encourage them to face setbacks in a similar way.
- **Share Joys**: Talk about the positive effects of reduced alcohol, like improved health or better sleep. Genuine enthusiasm can spark their interest.
- **Remain Humble**: Avoid acting superior or scolding them for their choices. Keep your tone approachable and understanding.

Being a real-life example of change can break through doubt. People see that an alcohol-free or moderate drinking life is not just possible—it can also be enjoyable.

15.13 Group and Community Efforts

Some individuals find it powerful to create or join group-based help for people wanting to quit alcohol. You could:

1. **Start a Small Meetup**: Invite a few friends who also want to stay sober or cut down for weekly check-ins. You might meet at a café or a public spot.
2. **Organize Activity Clubs**: A hiking club, board game circle, or craft group can give folks a sober social environment.
3. **Promote Online Events**: If in-person gatherings are hard to coordinate, schedule a weekly video call for sharing progress, tips, or just chatting.

4. **Team Up with Local Centers**: Some community centers or charities might welcome volunteers to lead workshops on healthy living or coping with stress.
5. **Keep It Flexible**: Not everyone wants a strict program. A casual but supportive group can be a huge relief for those feeling alone.

These group efforts not only assist others but also reinforce your own reasons for staying committed.

15.14 Sharing Resources

There are many guides, hotlines, and websites that give free or low-cost assistance. You can be a "connector" by pointing people to these resources:

- **Local Hotlines**: Many regions have 24-hour lines for substance problems. Knowing this number can be a lifesaver.
- **Free Counseling**: Some workplaces or community centers offer short-term counseling. Encourage them to ask around or check online listings.
- **Reading Material**: Suggest books with practical steps or real stories of recovery. A short reading list can be more helpful than random internet searching.
- **Apps and Trackers**: List any apps that let users log their drinks, track cravings, or manage stress.
- **Informative Websites**: If you found certain sites that explained withdrawal or health effects clearly, share the links.

By being an information source, you give them more control over their own progress. Knowledge often reduces fear.

15.15 Staying on Your Own Path

A concern when helping others is that their setbacks might pull you down. Watch for signs you are getting overwhelmed:

- **Excessive Guilt**: Feeling responsible if they relapse is a sign you are carrying their burden.
- **Neglecting Self-Care**: If you have no time for your routines because you are always helping them, step back.
- **Returning to Your Old Habits**: Stress from trying to rescue someone can create urges for alcohol.
- **Emotional Drain**: Feeling constantly sad, anxious, or irritated because of their problems is a warning.
- **Needing a Break**: If you dread their calls or messages, you might need to set limits for a while.

If you notice these problems, do not hesitate to seek counseling or talk with a trusted friend. Helping does not mean sacrificing your own health.

15.16 Handling Multiple People Seeking Help

Sometimes, word spreads that you overcame alcohol issues, and more people start coming to you for help. This can be overwhelming. A few strategies:

1. **Group Advice**: If several acquaintances are looking for tips, you could organize a small meet-up or group chat instead of repeating the same guidance individually.
2. **Set Time Windows**: Let them know your available times for calls or texts, so you are not bombarded around the clock.
3. **Refer to Professionals**: Remind them of local resources. You are one person, and they might need more specialized support.
4. **Protect Your Space**: If some are only half-interested or constantly in crisis, you might have to limit contact to protect your own well-being.
5. **Share Written Materials**: Compile a short guide with the main steps you found helpful. Direct them to read it first, then ask more specific questions later.

Balancing the role of a helper with your own life is key to avoiding burnout.

15.17 Offering Hope, Not Miracles

Real improvement often takes time. You can give hope by mentioning realistic expectations:

- **Small Steps**: Suggest they focus on short goals, like reducing drinks per week or staying sober on work nights.
- **Talk About Process**: Explain that setbacks happen. What matters is learning from them.
- **Highlight Gradual Gains**: Energy, mood, and relationships can get better month by month, not always instantly.
- **Reject Perfection**: Let them know they do not need to do everything right away. Consistency is more important than sudden big changes.
- **Encourage Patience**: Emotional issues and health problems might take a while to heal fully.

Sharing realistic hope helps them avoid feeling like a failure if results are slow.

15.18 The Benefits of Group Service Projects

Another angle is to involve them in projects that help others. Sometimes, focusing outward can shift a person's mindset:

- **Community Volunteering**: Working at a food bank, cleaning a local park, or helping an animal shelter can give a sense of purpose without alcohol.
- **Peer-Led Workshops**: If you both have some experience, you might co-lead a session for newcomers on coping strategies.
- **Charity Events**: Participating in walks, runs, or simple fundraisers for addiction recovery charities can create positive energy.
- **Sharing Skills**: If they have a hobby—like painting—they could teach a small class. This keeps them busy in a good way.
- **Group Celebrations**: When a volunteer project succeeds, mark it with a meal or small outing that does not involve alcohol.

Engaging in helpful causes can uplift spirits and reduce the urge to drink.

15.19 Knowing When to Step Back

Sometimes, despite your best efforts, the person does not change or even takes a worse turn. If it starts harming your mental health or they show aggressive or toxic behavior:

1. **Set Boundaries**: "I can't talk right now if you are going to be hostile. Let's chat again when things are calmer."
2. **Seek Professional Guidance**: You might speak to a counselor about your concerns. They might have suggestions on how to handle the situation.
3. **Stay Safe**: If the person's behavior is risky or violent, you may need to protect yourself and possibly contact authorities.
4. **Recognize Your Limitations**: You cannot rescue someone who does not want help. Be kind to yourself about that truth.
5. **Leave the Door Open**: Let them know you care, but you cannot keep engaging if it is damaging you. They can reach out again if they decide to get help.

Stepping back is not giving up on them; it is understanding that you have limits too.

CHAPTER 16: MOVING ON FROM PAST MISTAKES

No matter how determined you are to quit or cut down on alcohol, you might carry memories or regrets from earlier days. Maybe you regret missed opportunities, arguments, damage to relationships, or even legal or financial troubles that happened because of drinking. It is normal to feel bad about these events. Guilt can remind you why you wanted to change in the first place. But if you let that guilt turn into constant shame or self-blame, it can make it harder to move forward.

This chapter focuses on how to face mistakes without getting stuck in them. We will talk about how to begin forgiving yourself, how to make amends if needed, and how to build a new identity that is not defined by your old habits. By learning ways to handle regret in a healthy manner, you can let your past guide you instead of drag you down.

16.1 Understanding Guilt vs. Shame

Before diving in, let's clarify the difference between guilt and shame:

1. **Guilt**: Usually arises from specific actions. You might think, "I did something wrong," or "I hurt someone." Guilt can be a sign you recognize the harm and want to do better.
2. **Shame**: Is deeper and more personal. It might make you think, "I am a bad person," instead of "I made a mistake."

Guilt can be productive if it pushes you to change. Shame, on the other hand, can be paralyzing. It tells you that your whole self is flawed, which might cause you to feel unworthy of improvement. If you find you have repeated thoughts like, "I don't deserve a good life," or "I'm a failure," you are likely dealing with shame.

Why It Matters
If you let shame take over, you may be more likely to return to harmful habits just to escape the pain of feeling "bad." By recognizing when you are in shame mode, you can interrupt it and remind yourself that everyone makes mistakes. The true test is whether you learn and grow from them.

16.2 Facing Regret Head-On

It may be tempting to bury your regrets or pretend they never happened. However, pushing them away can cause them to pop up when you least expect it—during stress, in dreams, or in random thoughts that spark cravings. A healthier approach is to look at your past actions honestly:

- **Write It Down**: Jot down the main events or behaviors you regret. Give yourself permission to be honest. Seeing them on paper can be hard, but it can also help you accept reality.
- **Name the Emotions**: Next to each regret, note how you feel—sadness, anger, shame, fear. Recognizing the exact emotion can make it more manageable.
- **Remind Yourself Why You Quit**: For each regret, think about how it led you to realize changes were needed. Perhaps you missed a child's event or drove under the influence. Those painful memories fueled your decision to get sober or reduce drinking.

Facing regret directly is often the first step in preventing it from controlling you. You can then move forward with a plan to heal and make amends where possible.

16.3 Making Amends Where Possible

If your past actions hurt others—friends, family, coworkers—you may want to consider making amends. This does not mean everyone will forgive you instantly, but showing genuine effort can help mend trust. Here are basic steps:

1. **Reflect on Who Was Harmed**: Identify the people affected by your actions or the harm you caused them.
2. **Plan What to Say**: Think about what you want to communicate: a simple apology, an offer to replace or repair something, or a promise to do better.
3. **Choose the Right Time and Place**: A calm, private setting usually works best. Surprising someone in a public place can make them uncomfortable.
4. **Be Genuine**: Say what you did wrong, why you are sorry, and how you intend to change. Avoid justifying your past actions with excuses.

5. **Listen to Their Response**: They might still be upset or need time to heal. Accept their feelings without pushing them to forgive right away.

Not everyone will welcome your apology, and that can be painful. Still, making amends is as much about your own growth as it is about seeking acceptance.

16.4 Forgiving Yourself

Even after others have moved on, you might still be harsh with yourself. Self-forgiveness can be one of the hardest parts of recovery. Some steps that might help include:

- **Inner Dialogue**: Notice if your mind is filled with thoughts like, "I'm terrible," or "I can never fix this." Try countering them with, "I made mistakes, but I'm taking steps to improve now."
- **Recognize Growth**: Write down the positive changes you have made—staying sober for a certain number of days, repairing finances, improving your health. Realizing your progress can soften self-criticism.
- **Practice Kindness**: Treat yourself as you would treat a good friend in the same situation. You would likely tell that friend, "You are trying hard, and you deserve another chance."
- **Stay in the Present**: Shame thrives on dwelling on old events. Focus on what you can do today to keep moving forward, whether that is journaling, taking a walk, or reaching out to a support person.
- **Seek Professional Help**: If guilt or shame is overwhelming, counseling can guide you through deeper methods of self-forgiveness.

Self-forgiveness does not mean denying the harm done. It means accepting that you cannot change the past but can build a healthier future.

16.5 Learning from Mistakes

Mistakes can actually be valuable guides if you look at them carefully. For each regret, ask:

- **What Led to This?** Did stress at work, certain friends, or negative emotions push you to drink too much or behave badly?

- **Which Needs Were Unmet?** Maybe you lacked healthy ways to manage sadness, boredom, or anger.
- **How Could I Handle It Differently Now?** Maybe you have better coping skills, a daily routine, or supportive contacts.
- **What Did I Discover About Myself?** You might have learned you are more resilient than you thought, or that you need certain environments to stay safe.

By turning past errors into lessons, you give them a positive role in your recovery story. Then, even painful memories can hold a spark of wisdom.

16.6 Building a New Identity

For a long time, you might have defined yourself as someone who drinks or who relies on alcohol to handle life. As you change, it is natural to wonder, "Who am I without drinking?" Here are ways to build a new self-image:

1. **Focus on Strengths**: List what you do well—maybe you are creative, compassionate, organized, or good at problem-solving. These traits can become part of how you see yourself.
2. **Try Fresh Activities**: We talked about hobbies and routines before. Each new skill you develop (like painting or gardening) can expand your identity beyond "the person who drank."
3. **Surround Yourself with Supportive People**: Being around folks who encourage your sober or moderate-living identity helps it feel real.
4. **Create Goals**: Aim for something that excites you, like finishing a course, improving your fitness, or planning a family trip. Working toward a goal reshapes your day-to-day focus.
5. **Celebrate (Mark) Achievements**: Whenever you reach a milestone (like staying sober for a certain span or handling a tough situation without alcohol), note it. Success stories become part of your new story.

A strong new identity can keep you from sliding back into old self-perceptions that feed harmful habits.

16.7 Handling Disappointment if Others Hold Grudges

Sometimes, family or friends do not let go of the past easily. They may continue to see you as the person you were when you drank heavily, or they may not trust you around certain events. This can be discouraging. Here's how to handle it:

- **Show Consistency**: Over time, people may change their view if they see your new, steady behavior.
- **Invite Them to Talk**: If someone is cold or distant, politely ask if they want to discuss how you hurt them. Listen without jumping to defend yourself.
- **Respect Their Pace**: Healing can take time. You might feel ready to move on, but they might still be cautious.
- **Avoid Resentment**: Feeling angry at them might trap you in more negative emotions. Focus on your own actions and patience.
- **Set Boundaries**: If someone's hostility or suspicion becomes too toxic, you might limit contact for your own well-being, at least until things cool down.

Remember that you cannot control others' reactions. All you can do is keep living in a way that shows real change.

16.8 Using Supportive Outlets for Emotions

Moving on from mistakes can stir up sadness, regret, or frustration. You need healthy ways to channel these feelings. Some outlets include:

- **Therapy or Counseling**: A trained professional can help you unpack complex emotions.
- **Support Groups**: Meeting others with similar experiences can reduce feelings of isolation.
- **Journaling**: Writing about your regrets, your goals, and your progress can clarify your thoughts.
- **Creative Expression**: Whether it is art, music, or writing short stories, creativity can release built-up tension.
- **Exercise**: Physical movement can lower stress hormones and bring a sense of relief or accomplishment.

These activities keep heavy emotions from piling up and pushing you toward self-blame or returning to old habits.

16.9 Communicating with Loved Ones About the Future

Instead of focusing on what went wrong, you can talk with loved ones about what comes next:

1. **Share Hopes and Plans**: Let them know your vision—whether it is to keep a steady job, rebuild family bonds, or adopt healthier routines.
2. **Ask for Their Input**: Maybe they have ideas on how to strengthen relationships or plan activities that do not involve drinking.
3. **Set Realistic Expectations**: Rebuilding trust takes time. Do not promise instant changes in areas like finances or emotional availability. Outline steps you are taking instead.
4. **Discuss Boundaries**: If certain triggers or topics make you uneasy, let them know. For instance, you might say, "I am not comfortable going to bars yet."
5. **Seek Collaboration**: If you share a household, plan chores, budgets, or leisure activities together. This teamwork can replace old patterns.

Shifting the conversation from past mistakes to future possibilities can lift everyone's spirits and steer them toward solutions.

16.10 Letting Go of Resentment Toward Others

It is not just about forgiving yourself—you might have anger toward people who did not support you when you needed them, or who judged you harshly. Holding onto that anger can keep you trapped:

- **Acknowledge the Pain**: It is valid to feel hurt if someone betrayed you or abandoned you.
- **Separate Their Behavior from Your Healing**: Their actions are on them. Your healing is about you.
- **Avoid the "Blame Trap"**: Even if someone else contributed to your stress, ultimately you chose how to react. Owning your part can help you move on.

- **Practice Compassion**: Sometimes, people act out of ignorance or their own pain. This does not excuse harm, but understanding it can reduce bitterness.
- **Consider a Process**: Letting go might take repeated efforts. Journaling or therapy can help you release anger in a safer way.

By letting go of old grudges, you free up emotional space to focus on building a life you truly want.

16.11 Recognizing the Difference Between Regret and Relapse Signs

Regret can sometimes stir up strong emotions, which might mimic the early signs of relapse. Watch out for:

- **Unhealthy Self-Talk**: "I've already ruined things, so why not drink again?"
- **Isolation**: You might withdraw because you feel unworthy of friends or family.
- **Seeking Quick Escape**: Feeling overwhelmed by guilt or shame can make you crave the old numbness.
- **Sudden Social Risks**: You might test yourself by going to places you used to drink heavily, possibly as a self-punishing move.

When you spot these signals, remember your coping strategies. Reach out for support. Remind yourself that hurting yourself more does not fix what happened in the past.

16.12 Maintaining Perspective Over Time

Healing from regret does not happen overnight. Some days you might feel on top of the world; other days, an old memory hits you hard. Here are ways to keep perspective:

1. **Use a Calendar or Tracker**: Mark the weeks or months since you last drank heavily. Look back occasionally to see how far you have come.
2. **Talk with Mentors**: Stay in touch with people who have been sober longer. They can assure you that rough patches are normal.

3. **Celebrate Progress in Other Areas**: Perhaps you got a job promotion, improved a relationship, or learned a new skill. These wins show that you are not stuck in the past.
4. **Practice Patience**: Emotional healing is rarely a straight line. Ups and downs do not mean you are failing.
5. **Look for Patterns**: If certain seasons or events stir up regret, prepare in advance by checking in with supportive friends or counselors.

As time goes on, the intense regret usually fades, replaced by more balanced feelings about what happened and who you have become since.

16.13 Choosing Positive Self-Talk

The mind can replay mistakes like an old movie, making you feel guilty each time. You can learn to replace negative mental scripts with kinder language:

- **Negative Thought**: "I ruined my life already."
  Replacement: "I made some poor choices, but I'm fixing what I can and building better habits."
- **Negative Thought**: "I'll never be forgiven."
  Replacement: "Some people may take time to trust me, but I can keep showing them I've changed."
- **Negative Thought**: "I'm too weak to stay sober."
  Replacement: "I have the strength to face challenges and I have shown it by sticking with my plan so far."

Changing self-talk can feel unnatural at first, but over time, it becomes a key tool in moving on.

16.14 Celebrating Growth in Healthy Ways

Old habits might have led you to reach for a drink to mark a special moment or relieve stress. Now, with regrets behind you, you can find new ways to recognize growth:

1. **Treat Yourself**: Buy a small gift, a useful gadget, or new art supplies—something that supports your new interests.

2. **Share with Friends**: Invite them for a simple meal or a picnic. It does not have to be fancy or involve alcohol.
3. **Document Achievements**: Maybe you keep a scrapbook or digital folder where you write or store pictures about successes.
4. **Plan a Future Goal**: Use progress as motivation to tackle a new target, like attending a class or starting a small business idea.
5. **Give Back**: Volunteering or helping others can also be a great way to mark personal progress.

When you see your own development clearly, regrets lose some of their power to drag you down.

16.15 Dealing with Lingering Legal or Financial Consequences

Some mistakes, like legal trouble or debt, might follow you even if you have quit drinking. This can cause ongoing stress or remind you of the past. Tackle these issues step by step:

- **Face Debt Directly**: Create a plan, possibly with a financial counselor, to pay it off gradually. Each payment is a sign you are fixing what went wrong.
- **Talk to a Legal Advisor**: If you have legal obligations, meet them responsibly and ask about ways to reduce penalties over time.
- **Stay Organized**: Keep track of due dates for fees or court appearances so you do not add more trouble.
- **Accept It as Part of Growth**: Paying off debts or fulfilling legal duties can be a daily reminder of the cost of alcohol misuse, but it also proves you are responsible now.
- **Seek Support**: If money stress or legal fear triggers anxiety, share it with someone you trust or a support group.

Long-term burdens may be annoying, but each step toward clearing them is also progress toward a freer life.

16.16 Allowing Yourself Moments of Pride

It may feel odd to be proud of yourself if you still regret past behaviors. Yet allowing small moments of pride can motivate you:

- **Acknowledge Daily Wins**: Did you refuse a tempting invite? Complete a task you used to avoid? Write it down.
- **Embrace Positive Feedback**: If someone says, "I see you are doing better," let that praise in. Resist the urge to dismiss it by saying, "Not really."
- **Remember the Journey**: Reflect on how you used to handle stress versus how you do now. Recognize the gap between then and now.
- **Stay Humble but Confident**: Pride does not mean bragging. It means recognizing genuine effort and improvement.

Confidence in your ability to move forward can help override the weight of old regrets.

16.17 Handling Triggers Linked to Past Mistakes

Sometimes, certain places, songs, or objects can remind you of painful incidents related to alcohol. These triggers might stir up shame or sadness. Strategies to cope:

- **Change the Association**: If a certain park reminds you of a bad event, create a new memory there—have a calm walk or a short picnic with a supportive friend.
- **Remove Physical Reminders**: If you have items in your home that bring back negative memories, consider donating or discarding them.
- **Prepare a Script**: If a trigger appears unexpectedly, have a mental phrase like, "Yes, that happened, but I'm a different person now."
- **Use Calming Techniques**: Deep breathing or focusing on a simple object nearby can pull you out of flashbacks.
- **Share with a Support Person**: Talking about what triggered you can lessen its grip.

Over time, triggers lose their power if you face them with new, positive habits.

16.18 Accepting the Unchangeable

Some consequences of your past might be irreversible—like losing a job you loved, damaging certain relationships permanently, or facing health issues. Accepting these can be painful, but it is part of moving on:

1. **Grieve the Loss**: It is okay to feel sadness or regret about what cannot be undone.
2. **Focus on What Remains**: Turn your attention to the people and opportunities still in your life.
3. **Build Something New**: If one career path is closed, explore another. If one relationship ended, invest energy into a healthier friendship or a family bond.
4. **Let Sadness Be a Motivator**: Use the knowledge of what you cannot get back as extra reason not to return to alcohol misuse.
5. **Seek Closure**: Even if the situation is final, you can write a letter you never send, expressing your regret, then keep or destroy it as a symbolic act of letting go.

Acceptance does not mean you are "okay" with the harm done. It means you acknowledge reality and choose to keep growing anyway.

16.19 Keeping Hope Alive

Overcoming mistakes and building a new life requires hope. Sometimes hope can waver if you focus too much on regrets. To keep hope alive:

- **Look at Role Models**: Read or watch stories of people who overcame major setbacks. This can inspire you.
- **Set Manageable Goals**: Achieving small successes often fuels bigger dreams.
- **Stick to Routines**: A steady daily routine can provide a stable foundation when your emotions fluctuate.
- **Use Positive Reminders**: Place a motivating quote or note somewhere you see daily.
- **Celebrate (Mark) Personal Milestones**: Every step forward—like an emotional breakthrough or a successful conversation—deserves recognition.

Hope is not about ignoring problems. It is about trusting that growth is possible despite them.

CHAPTER 17: STAYING MOTIVATED IN DAILY LIFE

It is normal for motivation to come and go. When you first stop or cut down on alcohol, you might feel a surge of hope or excitement. Over time, day-to-day routines can make that excitement fade. You may find yourself wondering, "Is this all there is now?" or "I've done well so far, but I am losing that spark." This chapter addresses how to maintain focus on your bigger goals. We will talk about practical ways to stay driven, even when life feels repetitive or stressful. We will also look at new angles to spark your interest, keep your mind fresh, and remind you why living without heavy drinking is worth it.

17.1 Why Motivation Fluctuates

Motivation often comes in waves. You might wake up one day feeling determined, and the next day you feel flat. Many factors influence this, such as:

1. **Stress**: Work pressures, family problems, or health concerns can drain your mental energy.
2. **Routine Fatigue**: Doing the same tasks every day with no variety can make you feel stuck.
3. **Lack of Clear Goals**: If you have reached a certain milestone ("I have been sober for a month") and do not set another target, you might lose direction.
4. **Emotional Ups and Downs**: Mood swings from hormonal changes, weather, or personal events can affect how motivated you feel.
5. **Social Triggers**: Friends who still drink heavily or new social situations can make you question your plan.

Recognizing these patterns helps you prepare. Instead of feeling surprised by a dip in motivation, you can accept it as part of a natural cycle and use strategies to get back on track.

17.2 Refreshing Your Goals

If you set a goal like "Quit drinking," you might achieve it, but then what? A single goal can run out of fuel once you reach it. Consider refreshing or expanding your goals:

- **Add Health-Related Targets**: Maybe you want to work on better posture, improve stamina, or learn about balanced nutrition.
- **Pick a Fun Challenge**: Try a physical activity you have never done before, like a short local race or a dance class. Working toward it can keep you excited.
- **Develop a Skill**: If you are interested in cooking, playing an instrument, or building things, set a mini-goal each month (like trying three new recipes or learning a simple tune).
- **Focus on Relationships**: Perhaps your aim is to spend more one-on-one time with a child, sibling, or parent. Plan small outings or weekly calls.
- **Plan Personal Growth**: You might want to read a certain number of books, take an online course, or practice a daily mental exercise.

When you have fresh targets, you remind your mind and body that each day is part of an ongoing process, not just about resisting alcohol.

17.3 Creating Short Bursts of Inspiration

A common mistake is expecting motivation to stay at a high level. Instead, look for small, daily sparks that keep you moving forward:

1. **Morning Pep Talk**: Take one minute after waking up to note what you are thankful for, or to repeat a short phrase like, "I am strong enough to stay on track."
2. **Visual Reminders**: Hang up simple notes or pictures in places you look at often. This could be a note on the fridge reminding you of how good it feels to wake up clear-headed.
3. **Check-In Points**: Schedule brief breaks during the day to pause, breathe, and remind yourself why you chose this path.
4. **Reward Yourself**: At the end of a sober or moderate-drinking day, do something pleasant—listen to a favorite song, watch a funny video, or spend a few minutes on a hobby.

5. **Track Small Wins**: Use a journal or an app to record each day you stick to your plan. Seeing a chain of successful days can boost motivation.

Short bursts of positive energy can bridge the gap between bigger accomplishments.

17.4 Keeping a Personal Inspiration Toolkit

Some days, you may feel too drained to muster motivation from within. Prepare a simple "toolkit" you can turn to:

- **Favorite Quotes or Songs**: Save a few lines that move you or a short playlist that lifts your spirit.
- **Quick Workouts**: A 10-minute walk or gentle stretch can improve your mood more than you might expect.
- **Past Success Reminders**: Keep notes about when you handled a tough moment without alcohol, or overcame a strong craving. Read them to remember you can do it again.
- **Support Contacts**: Make a list of a few people you can message or call for a quick boost.
- **Relaxing Audio or Scenes**: Some keep short recordings of ocean sounds or photos of calm landscapes. It might sound simple, but such items can lower stress quickly.

The idea is to prepare these items beforehand so you do not have to hunt for them when you feel low.

17.5 Exploring New Interests to Prevent Boredom

Boredom can kill motivation. When life feels bland, you may recall how alcohol provided quick excitement or relief. To counter boredom:

1. **Sample Different Activities**: If you are not sure what you like, try something short-term, like a free online class or a weekend workshop.
2. **Mix Up Your Schedule**: Change the order of your daily tasks or try a new route to work. Even small changes can refresh your outlook.

3. **Seek Social Fun**: Look for clubs, group sports, or meetups that revolve around shared interests rather than drinking.
4. **Plan Future Adventures**: Book a day trip, local tour, or short course. Having something on the calendar can keep you motivated.
5. **Invite Others**: Doing things with a friend or family member can make it more enjoyable and keep you accountable.

When you fill your time with stimulating or novel pursuits, the appeal of alcohol tends to fade because you have healthier options for enjoyment.

17.6 Handling Stress Without Losing Focus

Stress is a big reason why many people relapse. Learning to manage stress effectively is key to staying motivated:

- **Identify Stress Points**: List the main sources of stress—maybe finances, work demands, or family tension. Then think of small steps to reduce each one.
- **Maintain Boundaries**: If a situation or person frequently brings drama, limit contact or set guidelines for how and when you interact.
- **Practice Calming Methods**: Deep breathing, simple muscle relaxation, or quiet time with music can lower stress hormones.
- **Divide Tasks**: Instead of tackling a giant to-do list in one go, break it down into chunks so you can see clear progress.
- **Remember Past Victories**: Reminding yourself that you faced stress before and handled it without drinking can boost your confidence.

Stressful events will come and go. If you have routines for dealing with them, your motivation will not drop so sharply when life gets tense.

17.7 Staying Connected with Support Systems

We often talk about the importance of support networks, but it is easy to drift away once you feel stable. You might think, "I don't need meetings or calls anymore." That can lead to a slow drop in motivation. Here is how to stay connected:

- **Regular Check-Ins**: Schedule a weekly call with a friend or group member who understands your goals.
- **Share Achievements**: If you have made progress—like a certain number of sober days—let your support network know. They will cheer you on, which fuels motivation.
- **Attend Groups Periodically**: Even if you do not go to every session, drop in sometimes to keep that sense of belonging.
- **Offer Help to Others**: Supporting someone else can remind you why you began. It also makes you value your own efforts more.
- **Use Online Platforms**: If in-person meetings are tough, find an online forum or chat group. A quick post can help you see you are not alone.

Staying in touch with people on a similar path helps keep the motivation flame alive, especially when personal doubts creep in.

17.8 Turning Setbacks into Stepping Stones

No one has a perfect run of sober or moderate days. You might have a slip or go through an emotional slump. Instead of letting it crush your motivation, see it as a learning chance:

1. **Analyze It**: What caused the slip? Was it a high-stress day, a social event, or negative self-talk?
2. **Revise the Plan**: Adjust your routine or coping methods to reduce the same risk in the future.
3. **Practice Self-Compassion**: Scolding yourself too harshly can lead to giving up. Acknowledge the mistake, but remind yourself you are still on track if you keep trying.
4. **Share with Someone**: Talk to a trusted friend or group about the setback. Their perspective might help you see solutions you missed.
5. **Renew the Commitment**: Sometimes writing or saying out loud, "I am recommitting to my healthy lifestyle," can close the slip and move you forward.

Seeing setbacks as part of the learning curve can keep your motivation strong, rather than letting one mistake define you.

17.9 Finding Meaningful Activities

Staying motivated often hinges on feeling like your life has purpose beyond avoiding alcohol. Think about adding activities that feel important to you:

- **Volunteering**: Helping at an animal shelter, local charity, or youth center can give you a sense of contribution and keep your mind busy.
- **Creative Expression**: Writing, sketching, or making crafts can be more than a hobby—it can be a way to process feelings and share them.
- **Community Projects**: Joining local clean-up events, community gardens, or cultural gatherings can link you with people who share a desire to improve the neighborhood.
- **Mentoring**: If you are further along in sobriety, you might guide someone who is just starting. This adds meaning and keeps your own drive strong.
- **Spiritual or Personal Reflection**: If you have spiritual beliefs or personal principles, you can find groups or quiet times to strengthen those values.

When you see yourself doing tasks that matter—whether small acts of kindness or bigger community roles—you realize your new life is not just about "not drinking." It is about making good use of your time and talents.

17.10 Journaling for Ongoing Reflection

Writing can be a powerful motivator. It helps you track thoughts, progress, and goals:

1. **Daily or Weekly Logs**: Note highs and lows of each day or week. Were you proud of something? Did something lower your mood?
2. **Prompt-Based Entries**: Use questions like, "What did I do well today that supports my sobriety?" or "What challenged me, and how did I respond?"
3. **Goal Setting**: Write new goals at the start of each week, then revisit them later to see if you met them or need to adjust.
4. **Gratitude Lists**: Listing things you appreciate trains your mind to see positives, which helps keep you motivated.
5. **Write Letters to Future Self**: Compose a note to yourself a month or year from now. Remind future you why these steps matter.

Regular writing can reveal patterns, spark fresh ideas, and keep the bigger picture in focus.

17.11 Designing a Supportive Home Environment

Your environment can make or break motivation. If your home is cluttered, stressful, or full of alcohol reminders, it can be tough to stay driven:

- **Tidy Up**: A clear, organized space can help your mind feel less overwhelmed.
- **Remove Alcohol Triggers**: Keep any items related to heavy drinking out of sight or out of the house.
- **Display Your Goals**: Hang a small bulletin board with short quotes, pictures, or a calendar showing sober milestones.
- **Create a Relaxation Corner**: Put some cushions, a lamp, or a small speaker for music in one corner. This can be a place to read, meditate, or rest when stress rises.
- **Share the Space**: If you live with others, explain your goals so they can help by keeping certain triggers away or respecting your quiet times.

A home that aligns with your aims can give you a daily reminder of why you keep going.

17.12 Using Visualizations and Daydreaming Wisely

Visualizing positive outcomes can give you a boost:

1. **Picture Your Future Self**: Take a few minutes to imagine yourself a year from now if you continue on this path. Think about how you would look, feel, and act.
2. **Short Scenes**: If you have a specific event coming up (like a wedding) where you want to stay sober, mentally rehearse stepping away from the drinks table or chatting confidently with a non-alcoholic beverage in hand.
3. **Feel the Emotions**: Try to feel the pride, calmness, or happiness you would have in that scenario.
4. **Ground It in Reality**: Visualization is not magic. It just primes your mind to recognize and respond well in real situations.
5. **Beware of Unrealistic Fantasies**: Keep it modest and believable. You do not want to set yourself up for disappointment.

These mental exercises can remind you that the effort you put in today shapes how you will live tomorrow.

17.13 Setting Up Rewards (Without Alcohol)

It is common to celebrate (or "mark") achievements with a glass of something. Now that you want to avoid or limit alcohol, you can pick other rewards:

- **Healthy Treats**: A good meal, a fresh fruit smoothie, or a small portion of a favorite snack.
- **Comfort Items**: A new pair of cozy socks, a nice-smelling candle, or a soft blanket.
- **Experience-Based**: Going to a local event, a museum, a concert (minus the heavy drinking atmosphere), or a quick day trip.
- **Creative Gifts**: A new set of paints or a crafty kit that supports any new hobby.
- **Self-Care**: Scheduling a massage, a hair appointment, or a peaceful bath with soothing music.

Giving yourself small perks for progress keeps life interesting and deters you from wanting alcohol as a "treat."

17.14 Building a "Motivation Menu"

You can structure a short list of strategies that help you when motivation dips. Think of it like a menu: pick what suits the moment:

1. **Physical Activity**: A brisk walk, a dance to your favorite song, or quick jumping jacks to re-energize.
2. **Connection**: Calling a friend who understands, or reading positive messages on a support forum.
3. **Relaxation**: Five minutes of breathing exercises, a short guided audio, or simply lying down in silence.
4. **Creative Spark**: Doodling, writing a short paragraph, or playing with craft materials for a few minutes.
5. **Healthy Distraction**: Doing a word puzzle, reorganizing a small drawer, or watching a short educational video.

When you feel low, pick at least one activity from the "motivation menu." This proactive approach can stop a slump from turning into a crisis of self-doubt.

17.15 Tracking Your Wins and Lessons

Another powerful approach is to keep a log of "wins and lessons." A "win" is any positive action or result, big or small, and a "lesson" is something you can learn from a challenge or slip:

- **Wins**: "Had dinner at a restaurant with friends and chose a non-alcoholic drink," "Completed a busy workweek without feeling the urge to drink," "Helped a friend talk through their stress."
- **Lessons**: "Realized I get anxious if I skip breakfast," "Felt a craving when I was overtired—need better sleep," "Got upset with a coworker and wanted to drink, so I called a friend instead."

By noting these items weekly or monthly, you build a personal record of growth and solutions. Reviewing them can reignite motivation if you start feeling stuck.

17.16 Watching Out for Overconfidence

Sometimes, losing motivation does not come from feeling down; it comes from feeling overly sure. You might think, "I've totally beaten alcohol. I don't need these strategies." This can weaken your guard. Warning signs:

- **Skipping Support Meetings**: You decide you do not need any group check-ins or accountability, risking isolation.
- **Ignoring Routines**: You stop daily or weekly habits that used to keep you steady (like journaling or short workouts).
- **Testing Yourself**: Putting yourself in risky situations out of curiosity or arrogance.
- **Neglecting Emotional States**: Dismissing stress or sadness because "I can handle anything now."

If you notice these signs, remind yourself that balance is key. Confidence is good, but a little caution keeps you safe. Return to the habits that helped you succeed rather than throwing them away.

17.17 Staying Flexible as Life Changes

Your motivation methods at the start of your alcohol-free plan might not work forever. As life changes—new job, new relationship, or moving to another place—you might need different strategies:

- **Reevaluate Goals**: If you move from a busy city to a quieter area, maybe your health goals become more outdoor-focused. If you change jobs, your schedule might need a fresh routine.
- **Adapt to New Social Circles**: Different groups have different norms. If your new circle is more into weekend hikes rather than bar nights, your approach to socializing might shift.
- **Prepare for New Stress**: A new job or role might bring extra demands. Adjust your stress management plan as needed.
- **Keep Revisiting the "Why"**: Why you quit or cut back on alcohol may evolve. Maybe you started for health reasons but now you stay sober because of new personal growth goals.
- **Regular Reflection**: Every few months, ask yourself, "Are my methods still working? What do I need to tweak?"

Being flexible ensures you do not get stuck using outdated tactics or ignoring new realities.

17.18 Keeping a Future-Focused Mindset

One way to keep motivation high is to think about the future you want. This does not mean daydreaming all day. Rather, it means seeing your efforts as steps that form the tomorrow you desire:

1. **Set a Vision**: Picture where you want to be in 6 months, 1 year, or 5 years. Health, relationships, personal goals—how do they look?
2. **Link Daily Actions**: Each day, ask, "What small thing can I do that lines up with my vision?" This might be skipping a drink, finishing a piece of work, or having a real talk with a loved one.
3. **Use Visual Cues**: Some people create a simple collage or pinboard with words or images that represent their desired future. It is not fancy; it just reminds you of what you are aiming for.

4. **Accept Slow Progress**: The future is built daily. One small choice—like choosing water over beer, or practicing a skill for 10 minutes—adds up over weeks and months.
5. **Celebrate (Mark) Steps**: Each mini-goal reached is a building block. Acknowledge it briefly so you stay motivated to add another block.

Thinking ahead helps you see that your lifestyle choices today shape the life you live next month or next year.

17.19 Reviewing Reasons for Quitting in the First Place

When motivation sags, go back to the basics: why did you quit or reduce alcohol?

- **List the Problems Alcohol Caused**: Health scares, relationship clashes, money trouble, or legal worries. Recall how tough that felt.
- **Note the Improvements**: Better mornings, improved focus, saved money, calmer relationships. Remind yourself these positives came from changing your drinking habits.
- **Visual Check**: If you kept any photos or items from your worst drinking moments, glance at them to remember you do not want to return to that state.
- **Talk to People Who Saw the Old You**: A friend or family member might say, "You are so much better now. We're proud of you." That can fan the motivational flame.
- **Reflect on Emotional Gains**: Beyond physical benefits, you may have grown in self-control, self-respect, or peace of mind.

Revisiting your original reasons can restore that early spark you had when you first decided enough was enough.

CHAPTER 18: FINANCIAL AND LEGAL CONCERNS

Financial and legal problems often go hand in hand with heavy drinking. From buying alcohol regularly to dealing with job loss or legal fees from drunk driving charges, the costs can add up. Many people discover their bank accounts and credit lines are in worse shape than they realized once they start adding up the bills. Others might be on probation or facing court hearings. Handling these problems can seem overwhelming, but ignoring them can cause more stress and might trigger the urge to drink again.

This chapter aims to help you manage the financial and legal side of quitting or reducing alcohol. We will explore practical budgeting steps, how to handle debt, ways to find legal assistance, and how to keep a balanced mindset if you have ongoing legal obligations. By facing these issues head-on, you reduce the stress and uncertainty that can weaken your decision to live without heavy drinking.

18.1 Understanding the True Cost of Alcohol Use

Before making a plan, it helps to see how alcohol misuse drains resources:

1. **Direct Spending**: The price of alcohol can be high, especially if you prefer premium brands or frequent bars. You might have spent hundreds of dollars a month.
2. **Health Expenses**: Doctor visits, prescriptions, or hospital stays linked to heavy drinking can lead to big medical bills.
3. **Missed Work or Career Trouble**: Hangovers or poor job performance can result in lost wages, missed promotions, or job loss.
4. **Legal Fees**: Fines, court fees, higher insurance rates, or even the cost of bail if you face drunk driving or public intoxication charges.
5. **Damaged Property**: Some might have damaged a car or other property while under the influence, leading to repair or replacement costs.
6. **Spreading Financial Stress**: If family members had to cover your bills or fix problems you caused, it can harm relationships and create future tensions.

Seeing these costs in black and white can motivate you to stay on track. The money you save by drinking less can be redirected to better uses, from paying off debt to investing in personal growth.

18.2 Building a Basic Budget

A practical budget is the foundation of financial stability. If heavy drinking led to random spending, a budget helps you see and control where your money goes:

- **List Monthly Income**: Add up net pay from jobs, plus any side gigs, benefits, or other reliable income sources.
- **Track Expenses**: Write down all regular bills: rent/mortgage, utilities, phone, insurance, car payments, groceries, etc. Add average amounts for these items if they vary month to month.
- **Include Debt Payments**: If you owe money on credit cards, loans, or medical bills, note at least the minimum payments.
- **Plan for Savings**: Even if it is a small amount, try to save something each month. This safety net can help handle emergencies without panic.
- **Spot Problem Areas**: Look for spending you can reduce. This could be fast food, entertainment, or leftover alcohol expenses if you still occasionally buy more than you need.

Seeing a clear budget can calm money worries. When you know how much you have and where it goes, you feel more in control.

18.3 Tracking Your Alcohol Savings

One encouraging step is to note how much you save by not buying as much alcohol:

1. **Review Past Bank Statements**: Look at how much you spent on alcohol in an average month before you quit or cut down.
2. **Set Up a Separate Account**: If possible, move the amount you would have spent on alcohol into a savings account each week or month. This helps you see the real money you are saving.
3. **Use the Savings for Good**: You can use the extra to pay down debt, add to an emergency fund, or treat yourself to a healthy reward (like better groceries or a gym membership).
4. **Stay Motivated**: Every time you think about buying alcohol, recall that the same money could help you reach a more positive goal.
5. **Track Over Time**: At the six-month or one-year mark, total up your saved amount. This can be a strong reminder that change pays off literally.

Watching the numbers build can boost your resolve on days when you are tempted to slip.

18.4 Handling Debt from Past Alcohol Use

If you have debt because of alcohol-related spending or job loss, it is important to face it rather than avoid it:

- **List All Debts**: Credit cards, personal loans, payday advances, medical bills, or loans from friends. Knowing the full picture is key.
- **Check Interest Rates**: Some debts may have high rates that grow quickly if unpaid. Focus on those first.
- **Contact Creditors**: Sometimes, banks or companies will work out a payment plan or lower the interest if you explain your situation.
- **Consider Professional Counselors**: Non-profit credit counseling services can help you make a budget and negotiate with creditors. Be sure to pick reputable ones.
- **Avoid Quick Fixes**: Be cautious about "debt relief" offers that promise miracles. Do some research to avoid scams.

Paying down debt is not fun, but every payment you make is a step toward stability. Reducing the stress of owing money also makes it easier to stick to your healthy routines.

18.5 Rebuilding Credit and Financial Stability

Heavy drinking can hurt your credit if you missed payments or racked up big balances. Slowly rebuilding credit is possible:

1. **Pay On Time**: Set up automatic payments for bills so you do not forget. Late payments hurt credit scores.
2. **Use a Secured Card**: If your credit is really low, a secured credit card (where you pay a deposit that becomes your credit limit) can help you rebuild a positive history.
3. **Keep Balances Low**: Using less than 30% of your available credit can boost your score over time.
4. **Check Credit Reports**: In many places, you can get free yearly credit reports. Look for errors or old debts you can clear.
5. **Stay Patient**: Credit improvement takes months or years. But if you stay consistent, you will see progress.

Better credit leads to lower stress when you need a loan for a car or a place to live. It also reminds you that you are moving forward financially.

18.6 Dealing with Employment Issues

Alcohol misuse can cause job loss, demotion, or difficulty finding a new position. Here are some ideas to handle work-related problems:

- **Explain Gaps**: If you have an employment gap due to rehab or severe drinking periods, plan a brief, honest explanation like, "I had personal health matters to address, but I am now stable and fully available."
- **Show Improvement**: If you can, get a note from any treatment program or counselor saying you have made progress. This can help reassure an employer you are serious about change.
- **Ask for Second Chances**: If your old employer let you go but still values your skills, you might approach them politely after you have shown a period of stability.
- **Seek Training**: If you need to shift careers or get new credentials, look for affordable local courses or online classes. This can open fresh job paths.
- **Look After Work-Life Balance**: Once employed, be clear about not returning to old patterns. Keep healthy routines and guard against burnout, which can spark the urge to drink.

Losing a job due to drinking is tough, but with patience and a better track record, you can find work that supports your new lifestyle.

18.7 Legal Consequences: Where to Start

If you have legal trouble—like a drunk driving charge (often called DUI or DWI), public intoxication citations, or other offenses—you may face fines, required classes, or even probation:

1. **Comply Promptly**: Follow court orders or probation rules carefully. Missing deadlines or ignoring instructions can worsen penalties.
2. **Seek Legal Aid**: If you cannot afford a lawyer, look for free or low-cost legal clinics.
3. **Document Progress**: Keep records of your sober days, treatment program attendance, or group meetings. Judges often look favorably on people who show active change.
4. **Communicate Clearly**: If you are on probation and have restrictions (like a curfew or no alcohol), do not hide. Let your probation officer see you are serious about obeying rules.

5. **Plan Transportation**: If your license is suspended, figure out reliable ways to get to work or appointments without driving illegally. A rideshare plan or public transit can prevent more legal trouble.

Facing legal matters head-on can reduce long-term stress. Avoiding them only makes you feel cornered, which might push you toward alcohol for "relief."

18.8 Special Classes or Programs

Courts sometimes order alcohol education classes or treatment programs. Although it may feel burdensome, these can help you:

- **Learn Facts**: You might learn about how alcohol affects the body, legal consequences, and community risks.
- **Meet Others**: You may discover folks in similar situations, which can create a small support network.
- **Lower Future Penalties**: Completing these courses can show a judge you are taking responsibility.
- **Improve Self-Awareness**: Sometimes, these programs provide exercises or discussions that open your eyes to harmful patterns.
- **Ask Questions**: If something confuses you about legal rights or health matters, these programs can be a place to ask.

Try to approach these classes with an open mind. They might reinforce your motivation.

18.9 Insurance and Liability Issues

Heavy drinking can affect insurance costs, whether for health, auto, or life coverage:

- **Health Insurance**: Some plans cover treatment or counseling for alcohol use, but you need to check the details. If you are worried about cost, ask about payment plans or sliding-scale fees at local clinics.
- **Auto Insurance**: A drunk driving conviction might spike your car insurance rates. Over time, safe driving can help reduce them again.
- **Life Insurance**: Some policies ask about alcohol use. If you can show a stable period of low or no alcohol, you might get better rates.

- **Seek Expert Advice**: Insurance can be confusing. A licensed agent can explain how to improve your standing once you are sober.
- **Stay Honest**: Lying on insurance forms can void the policy later. Always give accurate information about your history and current habits.

Being aware of these insurance factors can help you plan your finances more accurately and avoid unwanted surprises.

18.10 Handling Court-Ordered Fines or Fees

If you owe fines due to alcohol-related infractions, try to set up a realistic payment plan:

1. **Contact the Court**: Do not wait for them to chase you. Ask if you can pay in installments.
2. **Keep Proof of Payment**: Save receipts or screenshots to prove you are meeting your obligations.
3. **Discuss Hardships**: If you truly cannot pay, some courts allow community service or other arrangements.
4. **Budget Adjustments**: You might need to cut back on non-essential spending for a while to pay court fees. This can be frustrating, but it is part of repairing the damage.
5. **Stay Updated**: If you move or change contact details, let the court know. Missing notices can lead to bigger fines or warrants.

Paying off legal debts can be a slow process, but each installment you make shows responsibility and helps you leave the past behind.

18.11 Dealing with a Criminal Record

A criminal record, such as a conviction for drunk driving or other alcohol-related offenses, can create long-term barriers. You may worry about background checks for jobs or housing:

- **Learn Your State or Country's Rules**: Some places allow records to be sealed or expunged if you meet certain conditions.
- **Fulfill Requirements**: Complete all assigned programs, pay fines, and maintain a clean record for a set period. This might let you apply for expungement.

- **Explain Positively**: If asked, briefly mention the conviction, state that you have turned your life around, and give proof (like certificates or references).
- **Seek Legal Advice**: A professional can tell you if it is possible to reduce the impact of the record or remove it entirely after some time.
- **Focus on Future Plans**: You cannot change the past, but you can show you are committed to being a reliable person now.

This area can be tough, but many people with past convictions still lead productive, meaningful lives after proving they have changed.

18.12 Avoiding "Money = Freedom to Drink"

When finances improve, some people slip because they think, "Now I can afford to party." Watch for:

- **Over-Rewarding with Alcohol**: Seeing better finances might tempt you to think you can "handle a few drinks." This can restart old habits.
- **Lifestyle Inflation**: Just because you have more money does not mean you should spend wildly. Keep living within means and direct extra cash to savings or important goals.
- **Keep the Long-Term View**: Remember how you used to spend on alcohol. How else can that money serve you or your family?
- **Plan Fun in Healthy Ways**: If you want to celebrate (mark) better finances, do it with non-drinking activities like a short trip or a new hobby kit.
- **Stay Accountable**: If you find yourself itching to buy alcohol with your extra funds, talk to someone in your support system.

Having more money is a plus, but it can also be a test of your resolve. Stick to the mindset that your finances are part of a better life plan, not an excuse to revisit heavy drinking.

18.13 Helping Family Members Affected by Your Past

If your alcohol use caused your family to spend their money or cover your debts, you might want to repay them or at least show gratitude:

1. **Acknowledge Their Support**: A simple "Thank you for helping me when I was struggling" can mean a lot.
2. **Offer to Pay Back**: If they covered your rent or bills, set up a fair plan to repay some or all of it if possible.
3. **Share Improvements**: Let them see you managing money better, so they feel relieved and less worried about future crises.
4. **Give Them Space**: Some might not want the money back; they just want you to stay sober. Respect their feelings but still keep them updated on your progress.
5. **Earn Trust Gradually**: Do not rush them to see you as fully "fixed." Consistent responsible behavior is the strongest proof.

By showing you understand the financial impact on them, you help heal those bonds and ease lingering resentment.

18.14 Practical Tips for Court or Legal Meetings

If you have to attend court or meetings with legal officials, the following can keep you steady:

- **Dress Neatly**: Show respect for the process by wearing clean, modest clothes.
- **Stay Polite**: Address the judge or officers calmly. If you are anxious, take a few slow breaths before speaking.
- **Speak Truthfully**: Lying can lead to bigger penalties. If you do not know the answer to a question, say so.
- **Bring Documents**: Copies of payments made, proof of program attendance, or letters of support can help your case.
- **Keep a Notebook**: Write down what the judge or officer says, especially if there are deadlines. This avoids forgetting details.
- **Check In with a Support Person**: Before and after your court date, talk to someone you trust. They can help you process the event.

Showing you are organized and sincere can make a positive impression on legal authorities.

18.15 Using Community Resources

Many towns or cities offer free or low-cost resources to help with financial and legal challenges tied to alcohol:

- **Job Placement Centers**: They can help you write a resume, practice interviewing, or find open positions.
- **Legal Aid Societies**: Staffed by volunteer or low-fee lawyers, they can advise on minor criminal issues, traffic offenses, or court procedures.
- **Local Support Groups**: Some groups focus on budgeting or deal with legal questions for those in recovery.
- **Libraries and Community Centers**: They might host workshops on financial literacy, debt management, or free tax help.
- **Religious or Non-Profit Organizations**: Some places of worship or charities have funds or programs for people in recovery who need short-term aid.

Do not hesitate to reach out. Asking for help is a sign of responsibility, not weakness.

18.16 Coping with Shame or Embarrassment Over Legal or Money Woes

It is easy to feel embarrassed if you have to appear in court or admit to being broke. These feelings can spark cravings to drink just to hide from shame:

1. **Acknowledge You Are Not Alone**: Plenty of people face financial or legal problems. It does not make you a hopeless case.
2. **Use Counseling**: Talking about guilt or anxiety with a professional can prevent it from overwhelming you.
3. **Focus on Solutions**: Each small step—paying a portion of a fine or closing a credit card—proves you are doing better now.
4. **Seek Peer Support**: In recovery groups, you will find many who have tackled money or legal issues. Their stories can comfort and guide you.
5. **Give It Time**: Rebuilding finances or clearing legal records is not instant. Patience is key.

Learning to face these struggles openly can also strengthen your resolve to stay alcohol-free, as you see the real-world benefits of your new life.

18.17 Balancing Payments with Personal Needs

If you owe money or have court fees, you might try to put every spare dollar into payments. While it is good to clear debts, remember basic self-care:

- **Keep Groceries a Priority**: A solid diet helps both body and mind. Living on junk food because you are paying debts too quickly can hurt your health and morale.
- **Plan a Tiny Leisure Budget**: If you do not allow yourself any enjoyment, you may burn out or get resentful and turn to alcohol.
- **Save Even a Small Amount**: Even if it is just a few dollars each week, having a small emergency fund can prevent panic if something unexpected happens.
- **Communicate**: If you have a family, talk about money openly. Share how much you plan to put toward debts, how much for bills, and what is left for small treats.
- **Avoid Getting Overwhelmed**: If you cannot pay everything at once, it is okay. Chip away steadily.

A balanced approach prevents new crises from derailing your progress.

18.18 Planning for Future Goals Once Debts Are Handled

Once you get a handle on immediate financial or legal hurdles, think about your long-term aims:

- **Emergency Savings**: Aim for a certain amount—often suggested is three to six months of living expenses.
- **Retirement Plans**: Even if you start small, a retirement account or pension plan can secure your future.
- **Education or Career Investment**: Saving up to go back to school or get certifications can raise your income later.
- **Home Goals**: If you dream of owning a home or moving to a better place, set that as a focus.
- **Family Security**: If you have kids, consider saving for their education or setting life insurance in place.

Building for the future is a powerful motivator to avoid slipping back. When you see real progress in your life, the thought of losing it to alcohol feels less tempting.

18.19 Accepting Long-Term Consequences

Sometimes, even after paying fines or debts, you might still have a mark on your record or find your finances limited. Accepting this can be tough, but acceptance helps you cope:

- **Acknowledge Reality**: Hiding from the truth (like a DUI on your record) only creates more pain. Accept it as part of your past.
- **Focus on What You Can Influence**: You cannot erase some things, but you can keep building a stable life that shows you have changed.
- **Seek Support Groups**: Certain groups help people with reentry or with finalizing old convictions. They can share tips and moral support.
- **Keep Pride in Gains**: You are more than your record or debt. Remind yourself of the positive changes you have achieved.
- **Remember That Time Brings More Options**: In many cases, restrictions or stigma lessens as you demonstrate consistent good behavior over the years.

Accepting the lasting marks is not giving up. It is deciding to move forward despite them and make the best of your situation.

CHAPTER 19: ADVANCED TIPS FOR UNCOMMON PROBLEMS

Most people who reduce or quit alcohol handle common issues like cravings, social pressure, or mood swings. Yet some situations can arise that are less common but equally challenging. These might be linked to physical conditions, personal beliefs, or very specific social settings. Dealing with these unusual problems can make you feel alone or misunderstood, especially if your support network has not gone through anything similar. This chapter offers strategies for these advanced or less typical challenges, so you do not feel stuck without solutions.

19.1 When a Partner or Family Member Still Drinks Heavily

You might be working hard to stay clear of alcohol, but what if someone in your home continues to drink a lot? This can create daily temptations or arguments. Steps to handle it:

1. **Open Communication**: Calmly explain your goals and why it is important for you not to drink. Ask if they are willing to respect boundaries, like not leaving bottles in sight.
2. **Set Household Rules**: If you share space, propose keeping alcohol in a separate cabinet or fridge. Ask them not to offer you drinks, even as a joke.
3. **Seek a Mediator**: If conflicts keep growing, consider asking a neutral party—a counselor, mutual friend, or family member—to help you both talk through the problem.
4. **Keep Personal Routines**: Make sure you have your own meal times and relaxation rituals that do not revolve around alcohol. This can help you keep your focus.
5. **Consider Bigger Steps**: In some cases, living with a heavy drinker can threaten your progress. You might decide you need a short break or a new living arrangement until you feel stronger.

19.2 Rare Medical Conditions and Alcohol Use

Some people have medical conditions that interact with alcohol in unusual ways. For example, certain genetic factors can change how the body processes alcohol, causing severe flush reactions or extreme hangovers. Others might have blood sugar issues that worsen with even minor drinking.

- **Consult a Specialist**: A regular doctor might know the basics, but a specialist (like an endocrinologist for blood sugar) can give targeted advice.
- **Keep a Symptom Journal**: If you suspect an unusual reaction, note what you drank, how much, and what symptoms followed. This helps doctors spot patterns.
- **Ask About Medications**: Some prescriptions can be dangerous when mixed with alcohol. Always ask your doctor or pharmacist about interactions, especially with mental health meds.
- **Be Realistic**: If you have a serious medical condition made worse by drinking, complete abstinence might be the safest route. Trying to "just have one" could lead to health crises.
- **Stay Informed**: Read reliable sources or connect with patient support groups for your condition. They may share coping methods that have worked for others.

19.3 Religious or Cultural Pressures

In some cultures, drinking is either strictly forbidden or strongly encouraged. If you are part of a religious group that bans alcohol, you might face guilt if you have a slip. If you are in a culture where drinking is the norm, refusing might raise eyebrows.

1. **Know the Guidelines**: Clarify what your faith or culture actually says about alcohol. Sometimes, traditions are misunderstood or taken to extremes.
2. **Respect Your Own Beliefs**: Even if your family has a certain view, remember you have personal choices too. If you decide to quit, that is your right.
3. **Seek a Faith Leader's Advice**: If you belong to a religious community, talking to a leader or guide might help you manage guilt or confusion.

4. **Blend Respect with Assertiveness**: In social gatherings, politely but firmly show you will not drink. Some cultures appreciate courtesy, so choose words that honor tradition without ignoring your boundary.
5. **Find Like-Minded People**: There may be others in your cultural or faith community who also limit alcohol. Connecting with them can reduce loneliness.

19.4 Living in a Remote Area or Having Limited Support

Not everyone lives in a city with multiple support groups. You might be in a small town or a rural place without many therapy options. While it can feel isolating, modern solutions exist:

- **Online Groups**: Many organizations host virtual meetings. You can join chats or video calls for advice and accountability.
- **Hotlines**: Free phone lines exist in many regions. You can call for immediate listening and support.
- **Local Professionals**: Check if a nearby clinic or even a local nurse can guide you to minimal-cost or free counseling options.
- **Build a Small Network**: If you only know one or two people who support you, keep them close. Phone or text them regularly for updates.
- **Use Mail or Phone for Accountability**: If you cannot visit a group, you can still keep a routine by mailing in progress logs or calling a sponsor daily.

Isolation does not mean you have to go it alone. Virtual resources and creative methods can fill the gap.

19.5 Alcohol Use in Professional or High-Pressure Fields

Certain professions—like entertainment, sales, or even high-stress corporate roles—might normalize drinking. You could feel extra pressure to "fit in" at business dinners or industry parties.

1. **Plan Ahead for Work Events**: Decide on a non-alcoholic drink to order. Practice polite ways to refuse drinks.
2. **Explain Briefly**: If asked why you are not drinking, say something like, "I have an early meeting tomorrow," or "I'm focusing on my health." Keep it simple.

3. **Find Allies**: There might be coworkers who also prefer not to drink or who respect your choice. Stand near them in social settings.
4. **Manage Stress Properly**: Some fields push you to work long hours. Use healthy stress coping methods so you are not tempted to rely on alcohol for relief.
5. **Use Soft Skills**: Show that you can still be sociable and fun without drinking. Engage in conversations, ask about people's interests, or talk about the job. Prove you are just as involved without the glass in hand.

19.6 Senior Adults Changing Drinking Habits

Older adults might have used alcohol moderately for years but now face medical issues that make drinking unsafe. Or they might realize that age-related changes in the body cause harsher side effects.

- **Talk to Geriatric Specialists**: Older bodies break down alcohol differently, and medication interactions can be riskier. A specialist can advise you best.
- **Rethink Social Customs**: If your retiree group meets at a lounge, suggest rotating to coffee shops or midday lunches.
- **Address Loneliness**: Some seniors drink out of boredom or isolation. Finding clubs for hobbies or volunteering can fill time more positively.
- **Mindful Medication Use**: Many older adults take prescriptions. Double-check with a pharmacist about any alcohol warning labels.
- **Stay Active**: Light exercise adapted to your abilities can improve mood and give you a daily routine that does not involve drinking.

19.7 Managing Alcohol Use After Weight-Loss Surgery or Major Health Interventions

Some medical procedures change how your body absorbs substances, including alcohol. After something like gastric bypass, you might feel stronger effects from smaller amounts.

- **Ask Your Surgeon**: They may have guidelines about alcohol. Some strongly advise no drinking at all post-surgery.

- **Track Reactions**: If you do choose to drink a small amount, be very cautious. Note if you get dizzy or unwell faster than before.
- **Nutritional Changes**: If you are on a strict diet, empty calories from alcohol can derail your weight or health goals.
- **Keep Emergency Contact**: Know who to call if you experience sudden issues after minimal drinking.
- **Stay Educated**: Join post-surgery support groups to see how others handle the issue.

19.8 Mental Health Conditions and Rare Triggers

Conditions like post-traumatic stress disorder (PTSD) or obsessive-compulsive disorder (OCD) can create unusual triggers for alcohol use. You might have nightmares, flashbacks, or repeated thoughts that drive you to seek escape.

1. **Specialized Therapy**: Look for counselors who handle both addiction and your specific disorder. Treatments like cognitive behavioral therapy (CBT) can help.
2. **Mindful Grounding Techniques**: If you feel a panic wave or obsessive thought, practice grounding—focus on senses (touch, sight, hearing) to stay in the present.
3. **Medication Management**: Some mental health meds help reduce severe symptoms. If you are on them, avoid alcohol to prevent dangerous side effects.
4. **Create a Crisis Plan**: Have a written plan: "If I feel an overwhelming flashback, I will call my therapist or do a breathing exercise."
5. **Support Groups for Specific Conditions**: Some online or local groups cater to those with PTSD, OCD, or other conditions, addressing how it intersects with alcohol.

19.9 Allergy-Like Reactions or Sensitivities

Some people develop hives, rashes, or breathing issues after just a little alcohol. These reactions can be mild or severe (like anaphylaxis).

- **Identify Allergens**: You might react to certain ingredients in beer (like wheat), or wine (like sulfites), rather than pure alcohol.

- **Test Safely**: Under medical guidance, you could test different products to see if there is a safe type—though complete avoidance might be simpler if any reaction is severe.
- **Carry Emergency Medication**: If your doctor advises you to have an epinephrine pen or antihistamines, do not leave home without them.
- **Read Labels**: Some drinks include unexpected ingredients, so always check. If uncertain, skip it.
- **Tell Friends**: Let people know you have this reaction so they do not accidentally give you a drink with hidden triggers.

19.10 Taking a Break from a High-Drinking Environment

Sometimes, the only advanced solution is a short or long retreat from your usual setting if it is toxic with alcohol. This might mean:

- **Visiting a Relative in Another Town**: Being in a fresh environment can help you reset.
- **Finding a Sober House**: These are group homes for people who want to avoid drinking. They can offer structure and support.
- **Asking for a Transfer at Work**: If the local culture at your office is too alcohol-centric, you might request a move to another department.
- **Traveling for a Program**: Some rehab centers or extended care facilities are out of state. A new location can remove triggers.
- **Thinking Long-Term**: If your entire community is based on drinking culture, you may consider moving to a place where you can grow more easily.

These big changes are not always simple, but for people surrounded by constant alcohol use, removing themselves might be the key to success.

19.11 High-Functioning Drinkers: Hidden Struggles

Some individuals do not miss work or lose social ties but still drink heavily. They might maintain a seemingly stable life—yet inside they battle health problems or private conflicts.

- **Self-Honesty**: Just because you keep up with responsibilities does not mean you are safe from harm. Heavy drinking can affect the liver, heart, or brain silently.
- **Medical Screenings**: Even if you function well, get regular checkups to catch any silent damage.
- **Acknowledge the Risk**: A single bad day might push you over the edge, leading to a big crisis. Recognizing that can push you to cut down earlier.
- **Look for Behavioral Clues**: If you get defensive about your drinking or you hide it from others, that is a sign of a deeper issue.
- **Consider Gradual Reduction**: If you are used to daily heavy drinking but still living normally, tapering might feel easier than cold turkey. Seek medical advice if you have physical dependence.

19.12 Mixed Substances: Alcohol with Other Drugs

Combining alcohol with stimulants, painkillers, or even casual recreational substances can create unique problems. You might not feel as drunk, leading to overconsumption. Or you could have a dangerous interaction:

1. **Know the Risks**: Some drug combos cause fatal outcomes, like opioids plus alcohol slowing breathing too much.
2. **Medical Oversight**: If you have used multiple substances, a detox with professional help is safest.
3. **Honest Disclosure**: Be open with doctors about all substances you use. They cannot guide you effectively if they do not know the full picture.
4. **Alternate Coping**: If you use other drugs for stress relief, find replacements—like exercise, therapy, or hobbies.
5. **One Change at a Time**: Some professionals might suggest tackling alcohol first, or they might recommend addressing both together. Listen to expert advice.

19.13 Sudden Life Events: Grief, Divorce, or Trauma

Uncommon does not mean rare. But major personal crises—like the death of a loved one, a messy breakup, or a natural disaster—can happen unexpectedly. They might reignite cravings or push you into new drinking patterns.

- **Anticipate Strong Emotions**: Sadness, anger, or confusion might tempt you to numb out.
- **Find Extra Support**: Increase therapy sessions, attend more group meetings, or stay with a friend if you fear isolation.
- **Seek Rituals for Healing**: Writing letters you never send, symbolic gestures (like planting a tree in memory of someone) can help process pain.
- **Avoid Rash Decisions**: In grief or shock, you might want to run away or completely change your life. Wait until you are calmer to make big choices.
- **Connect with Specialized Groups**: If you are dealing with grief, divorce, or trauma, look for groups that handle exactly that issue. They often have tips for not turning to alcohol.

19.14 Handling Surprise Triggers

You might have prepared for known triggers—parties, bars, certain friends—but advanced problems include sudden triggers you never anticipated: a certain smell, a random memory, an unexpected phone call.

1. **Pause and Breathe**: When caught off-guard, take a few slow breaths to steady yourself.
2. **Identify the Feeling**: Are you scared, sad, or angry? Naming it can reduce its intensity.
3. **Use Quick Distractions**: If possible, step away from the situation, call a friend, or play a quick phone game to break the mental loop.
4. **Review Later**: Jot down in a journal what happened and how you coped. Think of ways to handle a similar event in the future.
5. **Stay Open-Minded**: Surprises happen. Over time, you get better at handling them because you have tested and refined your coping methods.

19.15 Dealing with Painful Memories from Drinking Days

Another advanced issue is flashbacks or strong guilt over things you did while drunk. Even after you have mostly healed, a vivid memory might strike:

- **Revisit Chapter 16**: We discussed moving on from past mistakes. Refresh those steps.
- **Self-Talk**: Remind yourself, "I did wrong, but I have changed. I am not that person anymore."
- **Allow Emotions**: It is okay to feel regret or sadness for a moment. Then pivot to what you are doing today to live differently.
- **Share in a Safe Setting**: Telling a counselor or a trusted friend about the memory can lessen its power.
- **Keep Building Your Present**: Each day of healthier living chips away at the hold old regrets have on you.

19.16 Technology Overload and Social Triggers

In modern life, social media or the internet might bring advanced triggers: pictures of old party days, ads for alcohol, or "drinking challenge" videos. This can feel overwhelming:

1. **Curate Your Feeds**: Unfollow or mute accounts that glorify heavy drinking. Instead, follow health or inspiring pages.
2. **Use Apps Wisely**: Some apps can block or limit social media after a certain time, reducing late-night impulses.
3. **Check Ads Settings**: Many social platforms let you control ad preferences to reduce alcohol-related ads.
4. **Protect Your Energy**: Do not argue online with people who mock sobriety or push you. Log off or block them.
5. **Replace Time Online**: If you used to spend hours browsing party photos, put that time into a hobby or reading a helpful article.

19.17 Dealing with Instability or Homelessness

In some cases, alcohol misuse leads to losing stable housing. Finding a home or staying sheltered can be the biggest advanced challenge of all.

- **Emergency Shelters**: Seek local shelters. Some have specific programs for substance misuse.
- **Social Services**: Ask about transitional housing or grants. Non-profit groups can guide you on how to get back on your feet.

- **Prioritize Safety**: If you are in a dangerous situation, focus on immediate shelter and contacting help lines.
- **Look for Rehab Tied to Housing**: Some rehab centers offer structured living arrangements that also provide therapy.
- **Rebuild Step-by-Step**: Once you have a safe place, you can focus again on managing triggers and finding stable work.

19.18 Co-Occurring Disorders with Pain or Chronic Illness

Living with chronic pain or an illness that makes daily life tough might push you to use alcohol for quick relief. This is another advanced issue:

1. **Pain Management Specialists**: They might provide non-addictive meds, physical therapy, or other methods to reduce pain without alcohol.
2. **Therapeutic Movement**: Gentle exercise like swimming or stretching can ease certain pains if done safely.
3. **Mental Coping**: Techniques like mindfulness or short relaxation sessions can help you endure pain spikes.
4. **Avoid Mixing Meds**: If you have strong painkillers, mixing them with alcohol can be life-threatening.
5. **Honesty with Doctors**: Let them know you quit or cut back on alcohol so they can adjust your treatment plan effectively.

19.19 High Levels of Anxiety About Social Stigma

Some folks who stop drinking feel constant worry about being labeled "the sober one" in social circles. This can lead to advanced anxiety:

- **Positive Spin**: Instead of seeing "sober" as weird, embrace it as a sign of strength and health.
- **Selective Sharing**: You do not have to announce you quit alcohol to everyone. Sometimes, a simple "I'm not drinking tonight" is enough.
- **Seek Balanced Circles**: Over time, find people who accept you for who you are. Real friends do not judge you for not drinking.
- **Distract from the Topic**: If people pry, redirect with another subject—ask about their hobbies or mention a current event.
- **Professional Advice**: If social anxiety is extreme, therapy can teach you methods to handle scrutiny without panic.

CHAPTER 20: LOOKING FORWARD AND STAYING ON TRACK

You have reached the final chapter of this comprehensive guide. By now, you have explored the reasons behind problem drinking, learned about withdrawal, formed new routines, tackled social and financial issues, and even looked at advanced challenges that can arise. The question remains: how do you keep all this progress going for the long haul? Many people do well for a few months but then lose momentum. Others might face an unexpected stressor years later and wonder how to hold steady. This final section will offer practical reminders and guiding principles for long-term stability.

20.1 Embracing the Idea of Ongoing Growth

Real change is not a one-time event. It is more like a continuing process. After the initial excitement of quitting or cutting down fades, you settle into daily life. This is where small habits and consistent choices matter most:

- **Stay Curious**: Keep learning about health, self-care, or personal development. Each new insight can refresh your determination.
- **Expect Evolution**: As time passes, your goals and lifestyle might shift. Stay flexible and update your routines as needed.
- **Avoid Overconfidence**: Believing you are "done" can lead to risky complacency. A humble awareness that vigilance is needed helps prevent slips.
- **Seek Fresh Inspiration**: Read new books, join local events, or watch uplifting stories to spark motivation.
- **Share Knowledge**: Teaching others or sharing your story can remind you of why you keep going.

Ongoing growth means you never fully "finish." Instead, each day you get stronger in your new, healthier way of living.

20.2 Making Your Daily Habits Non-Negotiable

By now, you likely have a set of daily or weekly habits—like morning stretches, mindful breaks, or meal planning—that keep you stable. Protect these habits:

1. **Block Out Time**: Treat them like appointments. For instance, if you do a quick walk each evening, do not let random invites push it aside without reason.
2. **Simplify**: Make sure each habit is not too complex. If it takes an hour to do your routine, you might skip it when busy. Keep it short and doable.
3. **Combine Tasks**: Pair tasks if needed. For example, do your mindful breathing while waiting for water to boil.
4. **Get Support**: Tell friends or family about these habits. They can remind you or join you.
5. **Revise If Needed**: If a habit becomes stale, tweak it. Maybe instead of writing a journal at night, you do it in the morning.

Non-negotiable habits are your foundation. Even if you feel unmotivated, following them keeps you anchored.

20.3 Regular Check-Ins with Yourself

Take a moment each week or month to step back and assess how things are going:

- **What's Working?** Maybe you have found it easy to avoid cravings lately or you enjoy your new hobby.
- **What's Hard?** Identify any area that feels shaky, like social pressures or money stress.
- **Adjust**: Think of ways to handle the hard spots—maybe schedule a chat with a counselor or change your budget plan.
- **Celebrate (Mark) Growth**: Give yourself credit for any small victories. That might include stable relationships, better health, or new achievements at work.
- **Look Ahead**: Set a short goal for the next period, like finishing a small project or maintaining a certain exercise routine.

These check-ins prevent you from drifting on autopilot.

20.4 Staying Active in a Support Community

Even if you feel you no longer need support meetings every week, remaining part of a group can maintain your focus:

1. **Attend Occasionally**: Showing up once a month (online or in-person) keeps you connected and reminds you of the principles you have learned.
2. **Offer Guidance**: If you are further along, share tips with newcomers. This not only helps them but also solidifies your own resolve.
3. **Stay Updated**: Groups or forums may share new findings, local events, or changes in substance use laws that could affect you.
4. **Prevent Isolation**: If a crisis hits, you already have a network in place instead of trying to rebuild from scratch.
5. **Enjoy Non-Drinking Social Life**: Some support circles plan get-togethers or recreational events that do not include alcohol.

A light connection to a community can act as a safety net.

20.5 Adapting to Major Life Changes

Over the years, your life might shift: marriage, parenthood, job changes, or moving. Each big change can unsettle your routines:

- **Recognize Stress**: Even positive changes like a wedding can create pressure or distract from self-care.
- **Plan for Routines**: If you move, figure out how to keep or rebuild your daily healthy habits in the new environment.
- **Communicate**: If you get married or move in with someone, let them know about your non-drinking boundaries.
- **Stay Flexible**: You might need to shorten or modify your routine if your schedule changes. Aim to keep the core elements.
- **Watch for Emotional Ups and Downs**: A new job or a child can lead to joy and exhaustion. Manage both so you do not slip back to old coping methods.

Life changes do not have to derail you if you prepare mentally and practically.

20.6 Protecting Your Physical Health Over Time

As you maintain a life with less or no alcohol, focusing on long-term health can help you stay on course:

- **Regular Checkups**: Keep scheduling doctor or dentist visits. If you had any alcohol-related issues before (liver or heart concerns), continue monitoring them.
- **Nutrition Updates**: Over time, your dietary needs might change. Listen to your body and adjust.
- **Exercise Variation**: If you grow bored of one activity, try something new—like swimming, yoga, or a group class.
- **Mind-Body Connection**: Explore simple relaxation methods like breathing exercises, nature walks, or gentle stretching to reduce stress hormones.
- **Keep Hydrated**: Even after years of no heavy drinking, staying hydrated helps bodily processes and keeps energy levels steady.

Good health is an ongoing project, not a one-time fix.

20.7 Keeping Emotional Health in Balance

Long-term sobriety or moderation does not automatically solve all emotional problems. You may still face everyday conflicts, sadness, or unexpected anxieties:

1. **Therapy Tune-Ups**: Checking in with a counselor every so often can prevent small issues from growing.
2. **Watch for Warning Signals**: If you feel you are snapping at people or have trouble sleeping, it might be time to revisit coping methods.
3. **Journaling or Art**: Maintaining an outlet for emotions can clear mental clutter.
4. **Social Connections**: Spend time with friends who uplift you. Strong relationships can buffer stress.
5. **Seek Fun**: True emotional wellness includes moments of laughter and simple pleasures—like playing a game or enjoying a favorite pastime.

20.8 Avoiding the Myth of Being "Cured"

Some might say, "I do not have a problem anymore, so I am cured." While it is true you may have overcome major hurdles, alcohol dependence can sneak back if you ignore the basics:

- **Stay Humble**: Keep habits that support your choice, rather than thinking you will never be tempted again.
- **Look Out for Substitutes**: Sometimes, people swap alcohol for gambling, overeating, or other habits. Keep an eye on these.
- **Continue Learning**: Reading new studies or listening to experts can keep your mind fresh.
- **Check on Old Triggers**: Visit old triggers in your mind once in a while. Are they still triggers, or have you formed new associations?
- **Accept That Vigilance Is Normal**: This does not mean living in fear. It means caring for your well-being consistently.

20.9 Future Planning: Small Goals and Dreams

Setting goals gives you a sense of forward motion. They do not need to be huge, but they should align with your new, healthier self.

- **Career Moves**: Maybe you want to pick up a certification or change fields entirely.
- **Family Plans**: If you dream of having children, or you want to spend more time with relatives, plan how to make that happen.
- **Creative Ventures**: If you have a craft or art skill, think about selling your work or joining local fairs.
- **Long-Term Projects**: Some people find purpose in projects like restoring a classic car, writing a book, or learning advanced cooking.
- **Personal Milestones**: You could aim to run a 5K or set aside money for a special trip. Each step you take reaffirms the life you chose without alcohol dominating.

These goals keep your mind active and remind you that a healthier life opens new doors.

20.10 Handling Relapse If It Occurs

Even with the best plans, relapse can happen. Some go years without drinking, then slip during a tough time. The key is how you respond:

1. **Stop the Damage Early**: If you have a slip, do not say, "Oh well, I failed," and binge for days. Recognize it, stop, and reach out for help.
2. **Analyze the Trigger**: What led to the relapse? Was it stress, complacency, or a major life crisis?
3. **Revisit Strategies**: Use the methods from earlier chapters—focus on coping skills, daily habits, or a meeting with your support group.
4. **No Shame Spiral**: Feeling deep shame only feeds more harmful behavior. Acknowledge the error, but keep your identity as someone who can still recover.
5. **Seek Fresh Support**: Sometimes a counselor or friend can help you see blind spots you missed.

Relapse does not wipe out all your progress. It is an obstacle you can overcome, learning from it to strengthen your path.

20.11 Passing On Your Knowledge

One way to stay on track is to share what you have learned. Teaching or guiding others can cement your own resolve:

- **Mentor a Newcomer**: In a support group, volunteer to help someone who just started.
- **Community Talks**: Some local groups invite people in recovery to speak briefly. Telling your story can inspire listeners.
- **Online Support**: Join an online forum and respond to questions. You might have a perspective that helps.
- **Family Education**: If younger relatives or friends are at risk of heavy drinking, gently explain what you know in an honest, relatable way.
- **Create Resources**: If you like writing, you could make a short blog or collection of tips. If you like speaking, maybe record short audio clips.

Contributing to others' growth reminds you daily why your own stability matters.

20.12 Preparing for Holidays and Anniversaries

Certain dates—like holidays or personal anniversaries—can bring nostalgic thoughts of partying with alcohol or sadness about memories. Plan ahead:

1. **Host Sober Events**: Invite people to a potluck or game night where alcohol is not the focus.
2. **Create New Traditions**: If you used to have a drinking tradition on a holiday, replace it with something fresh—like an outdoor activity or a shared hobby.
3. **Invite an Ally**: Ask a sober friend or a supportive relative to attend events with you so you do not feel alone.
4. **Limit Time**: If you are attending a party, decide to leave after a certain point if you notice the drinking culture ramping up.
5. **Reward Yourself**: Each holiday handled well is a reminder of your growth. Mark that success in a small, meaningful way.

20.13 Using Technology Mindfully

We live in a digital world. Apps, trackers, and online connections can keep you focused—or they can distract you. Find a balance:

- **Recovery Apps**: Log your sober days, track cravings, or connect with a daily motivational tip.
- **Scheduling Tools**: Calendar reminders for therapy, group meetings, or even water breaks can help maintain routine.
- **Avoid Over-Scrolling**: If social media triggers envy or invites, limit your time on it.
- **Stay Realistic**: No app can replace human support, but it can be a handy addition.
- **Check Privacy**: If you share personal data with an app or group, ensure it is secure.

20.14 Financial Goals for the Future

Earlier chapters discussed handling debts. Now, focus on positive financial goals:

1. **Emergency Fund**: Aim for at least a small cushion for unexpected costs.
2. **Skill Upgrade**: Invest in short courses to advance your career, leading to better pay or satisfaction.
3. **Plan for Big Dreams**: Maybe you want to take a special trip or save for a house. Start small, but stay consistent.
4. **Give Back**: Some people donate a little to causes that matter to them. This can bring a sense of purpose.
5. **Stay Accountable**: Share your money goals with a trusted friend or partner, so you both stay on track.

When you see money being used for growth and not for alcohol, it strengthens your commitment.

20.15 Keeping Relationships Strong

Recovery often repairs old wounds, but you need ongoing effort to maintain harmony:

- **Open Communication**: Keep talking about needs, feelings, and triggers. Do not wait until problems explode.
- **Apologize Quickly**: If you slip up and speak harshly, apologize. Old resentments can resurface if not handled swiftly.
- **Show Appreciation**: Regularly thank family or friends who stood by you. Feeling valued can keep them supportive.
- **Respect Their Boundaries**: Loved ones might have worries from past times. Patience and consistent good behavior can rebuild trust.
- **Plan Activities Together**: Make time for shared experiences that do not involve alcohol—like day trips, picnics, or watching a series together.

Good relationships act as a buffer against cravings and negative thoughts.

20.16 Balancing Work, Leisure, and Personal Growth

Some people who stop drinking throw themselves into work or a new hobby too intensely. Balance matters:

1. **Check Overwork**: Even if you love your job, constant work can cause burnout, which can lead to relapse.
2. **Leave Space for Leisure**: Unstructured fun—reading, mild sports, or creative tasks—keeps stress down.
3. **Try New Skills**: If you tried one hobby and got bored, sample another. Growth keeps your mind engaged.
4. **Time-Management**: Use simple tools to ensure you do not neglect personal time or relationships.
5. **Celebrate (Mark) Milestones**: If you get a promotion or finish a big project, acknowledge it in a healthy way.

20.17 Nurturing a Sense of Purpose

One big reason people stick to healthier habits is having a cause or mission that motivates them:

- **Volunteer**: Helping at a food bank, animal shelter, or youth program can give you purpose.
- **Join Community Initiatives**: This might be a local improvement effort, a clean-up day, or a charity run.
- **Mentor Younger Folks**: Even informal guidance to teenagers in your neighborhood can make a difference.
- **Plant Something**: Gardening or growing a tree can be symbolic of your new start and can be deeply satisfying.
- **Support a Cause You Believe In**: If you are passionate about the environment, education, or health, find ways to contribute.

When you feel your life has value beyond yourself, the pull to drink may lose power.

20.18 Respecting and Safeguarding Your Boundaries

Long-term success means not letting people or events push you into unsafe zones:

1. **Practice Saying "No"**: This might be to a party invite or an extra task at work if you are exhausted.
2. **Limit Draining Relationships**: If someone constantly disrespects your boundaries, reduce contact if you can.
3. **Trust Your Instincts**: If a situation feels off or triggers old urges, leave or seek help.
4. **Ask for Space**: Sometimes you need time alone to refocus. Let close ones know it is not personal.
5. **Review Boundaries Often**: Over time, your comfort levels may expand or shrink. Adjust accordingly.

Boundaries are a form of self-respect and self-protection.

20.19 Giving Yourself Credit for Hard Work

Many people in long-term recovery forget how far they have come. They focus on future goals and never pause to appreciate their strength.

- **Reflect Annually**: On the date you quit or decided to reduce, look back at the major changes you have achieved.
- **Keep Tokens**: Some keep a simple coin or note from the day they started the new life. Seeing it can spark gratitude.
- **Talk to Loved Ones**: They may share how proud they are or how they have seen your progress. Listen and accept it.
- **Write It Down**: Pen a short reflection on the difference between your past and present self.
- **Stay Grateful**: Being thankful for the improvements does not mean you forget the effort. It just recognizes the positive outcome.

20.20 Summary

Looking forward and staying on track is about more than "not drinking." It is about weaving your healthier choices into every aspect of life—your relationships, your work, your goals, and your sense of self. By treating growth as an ongoing process, keeping daily habits strong, and adapting to new life phases, you keep your progress alive. You also remain prepared for any curveballs life throws.

In this final chapter, we covered strategies to keep momentum, handle major life changes, and find meaning in everyday living. We talked about staying humble, checking in with yourself, and remaining part of a support network. We stressed the importance of setting future goals, handling setbacks if they occur, and embracing a purposeful life that goes beyond alcohol avoidance.

The path ahead is yours to shape. You have learned about the body, mind, emotions, social dynamics, and practical concerns related to alcohol use. Now, it is time to put this knowledge into daily action. Each decision—big or small—builds the stable foundation you need. Whether you are just starting or you have been on this road for a while, remember that consistent effort, good support, and self-compassion are the pillars of real change. You can continue growing, enjoying life, and remaining free from the burdens heavy alcohol use once placed on you. With these tools and insights, you stand ready to create the future you want—one step at a time.

_____

_____

www.ingramcontent.com/pod-product-compliance
Lightning Source LLC
LaVergne TN
LVHW012104070526
838202LV00056B/5620